WEST-E 0856 Health and Fitness
Teacher Certification Exam

By: Sharon Wynne, M.S.
Southern Connecticut State University

"And, while there's no reason yet to panic, I think it's only prudent that we make preparations to panic."

XAMonline, INC.
Boston

Copyright © 2008 XAMonline, Inc.
All rights reserved. No part of the material protected by this copyright notice may be reproduced or utilized in any form or by any means, electronic or mechanical, including photocopying, recording or by any information storage and retrievable system, without written permission from the copyright holder.

To obtain permission(s) to use the material from this work for any purpose including workshops or seminars, please submit a written request to:

XAMonline, Inc.
21 Orient Ave.
Melrose, MA 02176
Toll Free 1-800-509-4128
Email: info@XAMonline.com
Web www.xamonline.com
Fax: 1-781-662-9268

Library of Congress Cataloging-in-Publication Data

Wynne, Sharon A.
 Physical Education 10091: Teacher Certification / Sharon A. Wynne. -2nd ed.
 ISBN 978-1-60787-637-3
  1. Physical Education 10091 2. Study Guides. 3. West-E
   4. Teachers' Certification & Licensure. 5. Careers

Disclaimer:
The opinions expressed in this publication are the sole works of XAMonline and were created independent of the National Education Association, Educational Testing Service, any State Department of Education, National Evaluation Systems or other testing affiliates.

Between the time of publication and printing, state specific standards as well as testing formats and website information may change that is not included in part or in whole within this product. Sample test questions are developed by XAMonline and reflect similar content as on actual tests; however, they are not former tests. XAMonline assembles content that aligns with state standards but makes no claims nor guarantees teacher candidates a passing score. Numerical scores are determined by testing companies such as NES or ETS and then are compared with individual state standards. A passing score varies from state to state.

Printed in the United States of America œ-1

WEST-E Health and Fitness 0856
ISBN: 978-1-58197-637-3

TEACHER CERTIFICATION STUDY GUIDE

Table of Contents

COMPETENCY 1.0 FUNDAMENTAL MOVEMENTS, MOTOR DEVELOPMENT, AND MOTOR LEARNING 1

SKILL 1.1 Fundamental movements: locomotor, nonlocomotor, manipulative, and falling/landing movement skills; movement concepts such as body, space, effort, and relationship 1

SKILL 1.2 Growth and motor development: role of perception in motor development, such as in spatial movement relationships; neurophysiology of motor control; effects of motor control; effects of maturation and experience on motor patterns; biological and environmental influences on gender differences in motor performances. 3

SKILL 1.3 Motor learning: classical and current theories of motor learning; variables that affect learning performance; effects of individual differences on learning and performance 6

COMPETENCY 2.0 MOVEMENT FORMS 9

SKILL 2.1 Dance and rhythmic activities; dance forms, such as folk, square, and aerobic dancing; skill analysis of dance movements 9

SKILL 2.2 Gymnastics: stunts and tumbling, use of gymnastic apparatus, movement themes in educational gymnastics 12

SKILL 2.3 Games: game forms, including, invasion games; cooperative and competitive games; analysis of skills, rules, and strategies of particular games 15

SKILL 2.4 Individual/dual/team sports: analysis of skills, injury prevention and safety, rules and strategies, facilities and equipment, lifetime activities and recreational pursuits, adventure and outdoor pursuits, and the martial arts. The emphasis is predominantly on basketball, swimming, soccer, softball, tennis, track and field, and volleyball. Questions may also be based on other sports or activities commonly used in physical education settings 16

PHYSICAL EDUCATION

COMPETENCY 3.0 FITNESS AND EXERCISE SCIENCE 49

SKILL 3.1 Components: cardiorespiratory and muscular endurance, body composition, flexibility 49

SKILL 3.2 Conditioning practices and principles: frequency, intensity, time/duration, the role of exercise 51

SKILL 3.3 Human biology: anatomy and physiology, including identification of major muscles, bones, and systems of the human body and their functions; exercise physiology, including terminology, components of fitness, principles of exercise, roles of body systems in exercise, short- and long-term effects of physical training, relationship between nutrition and fitness 56

COMPETENCY 4.0 SOCIAL SCIENCE FOUNDATIONS 83

SKILL 4.1 History of physical education leading men and women, major issues, and events in the history of physical education; historical relationship of physical education to health and fitness 83

SKILL 4.2 Current philosophical issues: purpose of physical education; relationship between teaching and coaching; accountability; roles, benefits, and effects of competition 88

SKILL 4.3 Sociological and sociopolitical issues: cultural diversity, equity (Title IX, Individuals with disabilities Education Act, affirmative action), general educational issues 92

SKILL 4.4 Psychology: personality factors that affect participation, social-psychological factors that affect participation, cooperation 94

COMPETENCY 5.0 BIOMECHANICS 96

SKILL 5.1 Terminology: mass, force, friction and basic principles of movement: summation of forces, center of gravity, force/speed relations, torque 96

SKILL 5.2 Application of basic principles to sports skills 96

SKILL 5.3 Methods of analyzing movement and analysis of basic movement patterns: overhand throw, underhand throw, kick 101

SKILL 5.4 Methods of analyzing movement 107

SKILL 5.5 Analysis of basic movement patterns: overhand throw, underhand throw, kick 108

TEACHER CERTIFICATION STUDY GUIDE

COMPETENCY 6.0 HEALTH AND SAFETY 110

SKILL 6.1 Safety and injury prevention: general and specific safety considerations for all movement activities; fitness-related safety considerations, such as warm-up/cool-down, harmful exercise techniques, and environmental conditions 110

SKILL 6.2 Health appraisals and referrals: health-related fitness appraisals; personal goal-setting and assessment, such as Physical Best, President's Challenge, and Fitness gram; considerations related to the Individuals with Disabilities Education Act 117

SKILL 6.3 Liability and legal aspects: considerations of equipment, class organization, supervision, program selection 120

SKILL 6.4 Effects of substance abuse on performance and behavior 125

SKILL 6.5 Effects of substance abuse on physical performance 128

Annotated List of Resources for Physical Education 129

Sample Test 131

Answer Key 160

Rationales with Sample Questions 161

Rigor Table 162

TEACHER CERTIFICATION STUDY GUIDE

Great Study and Testing Tips!

What you study in order to prepare for the subject assessments is the focus of this study guide, but equally important is *how* you study.

You can increase your chances of truly mastering the information by taking some simple but effective steps.

Study Tips:

1. Certain **foods aid the learning process.** Food such as milk, nuts, seeds, rice, and oats help your study efforts by releasing natural memory enhancers called CCKs (*cholecystokinin*) composed of *tryptophan*, *choline*, and *phenylalanine*. All of these chemicals enhance the neurotransmitters associated with memory. Before studying, have a light, protein-rich meal of eggs, turkey, and fish. All these food release the memory enhancing chemicals. The better the connections, the more you comprehend.

Likewise, before you take a test, stick to a light snack of relaxing and energy boosting food. A glass of milk, a piece of fruit, or some peanuts release various memory-boosting chemicals and help you to relax and focus on the subject at hand.

2. Learn to take great notes. A by-product of our modern culture is that we have grown accustomed to getting our information in short doses (e.g. TV news sound bites or USA Today style newspaper articles).

Consequently, we've subconsciously trained ourselves to assimilate information better in neat little packages. If your notes are scrawled all over the paper, it fragments the flow of information. Strive for clarity. Newspapers use a standard format to achieve clarity. You can make your notes much clearer by using proper formatting. A very effective format is called the *"Cornell Method."*

Take a sheet of loose-leaf lined notebook paper and draw a line all the way down the paper about one to two inches from the left-hand edge.

Draw another line across the width of the paper about one to two inches from the bottom. Repeat this process on the reverse side of the page.

Look at the highly effective result. You have ample room for notes. A left hand margin for special emphasis items or inserting supplementary data from the textbook, a large area at the bottom for a brief summary, and a little rectangular space for just about anything you want.

PHYSICAL EDUCATION

3. **Get the concept then the details.** Too often we focus on the details and don't gather an understanding of the concept. However, if you simply memorize only dates, places, or names, you may well miss the whole point of the subject.

A key way to understand things is to put them in your own words. If you are working from a textbook, automatically summarize each paragraph in your mind. If you are outlining text, don't simply copy the author's words.

Rephrase them in your own words. You remember your own thoughts and words much better than someone else's. You will subconsciously tend to associate the important details to the core concepts.

4. **Ask Why?** Pull apart written material paragraph by paragraph and don't forget the captions under the illustrations.

Example: If the heading is "Stream Erosion", flip it around to read "Why do streams erode?" Then answer the questions.

If you train your mind to think in a series of questions and answers, not only will you learn more, but you will also lessen the test anxiety. You get used to answering questions.

5. **Read for reinforcement and future needs.** Even if you only have 10 minutes, put your notes or a book in your hand. Your mind is similar to a computer; you have to input data in order to have it processed. *By reading, you are creating the neural connections for future retrieval.* The more you read something, the more you reinforce the learning of ideas.

Even if you don't fully understand something the first time, *your mind stores most of the material for later recall.*

6. **Relax to learn, so go into exile.** Our bodies respond to an inner clock called biorhythms. Burning the midnight oil works well for some people, but not for everyone.

If possible, set aside a particular place to study that is free of distractions. Shut off the television, cell phone, and pager and exile your friends and family during your study period.

If you really are bothered by silence, try background music. Studies show that light classical music played at a low volume aids in concentration.

Instrumental music that evokes pleasant emotions is strongly suggested. Try just about anything by Mozart. It will relax you.

7. Use arrows not highlighters. At best, it's difficult to read a page full of yellow, pink, blue, and green streaks.

Try staring at a neon sign for a while and you'll soon see my point. The horde of colors obscures the message.

A quick note, a brief dash of color, an underline, and an arrow pointing to a particular passage is much clearer than a horde of highlighted words.

8. Budget your study time. Although you shouldn't ignore any of the material, *allocate your available study time in the same ratio that topics may appear on the test.*

TEACHER CERTIFICATION STUDY GUIDE

Testing Tips:

1. Get smart, play dumb. Don't read anything into the question. Don't assume that the test writer is looking for something other than what is asked for. Stick to the question as it is written and don't read things into it.

2. Read the question and all the choices *twice* before answering. You may miss something by not carefully reading and re-reading both the question and the answers.

If you really don't have a clue as to the right answer, leave it blank the first time through. Go on to the other questions, as they may provide a clue on how to answer the skipped questions.

If later on, you still can't answer the skipped ones . . . ***Guess.***
The only penalty for guessing is that you *might* get it wrong. One thing is certain; if you don't write an answer, you will get it wrong anyway!

3. Turn the question into a statement. Look at the way the questions are worded. The syntax of the question usually provides a clue. Does it seem more familiar as a statement rather than as a question? Does it sound strange?

By turning a question into a statement, you might spot an answer. It may also trigger memories of material you've read.

4. Look for hidden clues. It's actually very difficult to compose multiple-choice questions without giving away part of the answer in the options presented.

In most multiple-choice questions, you can often readily eliminate one or two of the potential answers. This leaves you with only two real possibilities, and automatically your odds increases to fifty-fifty with very little work.

5. Trust your instincts. For every fact that you have read, you subconsciously retain something of that knowledge. On questions that you aren't really certain about, go with your basic instincts. **Your first impression on how to answer a question is usually correct.**

6. Mark your answers directly on the test booklet. Don't bother trying to fill in the optical scan sheet on the first pass through the test.

Just be very careful not to miss-mark your answers when you eventually transcribe them to the scan sheet.

7. Watch the clock! You have a set amount of time to answer the questions. Don't get bogged down trying to answer a single question at the expense of 10 questions you can answer easily.

PHYSICAL EDUCATION

THIS PAGE BLANK

TEACHER CERTIFICATION STUDY GUIDE

COMPETENCY 1.0   **FUNDAMENTAL MOVEMENTS, MOTOR DEVELOPMENT, AND MOTOR LEARNING**

SKILL 1.1   **Fundamental movements: locomotor, nonlocomotor, manipulative, and falling/landing movement skills; movement concepts such as body, space, effort, and relationship**

LOCOMOTOR SKILLS

Locomotor skills move an individual from one point to another.

1. **Walking** – This form of locomotion has one foot contacting the surface at all times. Walking shifts one's weight from one foot to the other while legs swing alternately in front of the body.

2. **Running** – This is an extension of walking that has a phase where the body is propelled with no base of support (speed is faster, stride is longer, and arms add power).

3. **Jumping** – This involves projectile movements that momentarily suspend the body in midair.

4. **Vaulting** – It is coordinated movements that allow one to spring over an obstacle.

5. **Leaping** – This is similar to running, but leaping has greater height, flight, and distance.

6. **Hopping** - uses the same foot to take off from a surface and land.

7. **Galloping** – This is a forward or backward advanced elongation of walking combined and coordinated with a leap.

8. **Sliding** – It is sideward stepping pattern that is uneven, long, or short.

9. **Body Rolling** This involves moving across a surface by rocking back and forth, by turning over and over, or by shaping the body into a revolving mass.

10. **Climbing** - ascending or descending using the hands and feet with the upper body exerting the most control.

NONLOCOMOTOR SKILLS

Nonlocomotor skills are stability skills. These require little or no movement of one's base of support and does not result in change of position.

1. **Bending** - movement around a joint where two body parts meet.

2. **Dodging** - sharp change of direction from original line of movement such as away from a person or object.

PHYSICAL EDUCATION

3. **Stretching** - extending/hyper-extending joints to make body parts as straight or as long as possible.

4. **Twisting** - rotating body/body parts around an axis with a stationary base.

5. **Turning** - circular movement of the body through space releasing the base of support.

6. **Swinging** - circular/pendular movements of the body/body parts below an axis.

7. **Swaying** - same as swinging but movement is above an axis.

8. **Pushing** – It is an act of applying force against an object or person to move it away from one's body or to move one's body away from the object or person.

9. **Pulling** - executing force to cause objects/people to move towards one's body.

MANIPULATIVE SKILLS

Manipulative skills use body parts to propel or receive an object, controlling objects primarily with the hands and feet. Two types of manipulative skills are receptive (catch + trap) and propulsive (throw, strike, kick).

1. **Bouncing/Dribbling** - projecting a ball downwards.

2. **Catching** - stopping momentum of an object (for control) using the hands.

3. **Kicking** - striking an object with the foot.

4. **Rolling** - initiating force on an object to instill contact with a surface.

5. **Striking** - giving impetus to an object with the use of the hands or another object.

6. **Throwing** - using one or both arms to project an object into midair away from the body.

7. **Trapping** - without the use of the hands, receiving and controlling a ball.

CONCEPT OF SPATIAL AWARENESS APPLIED TO PHYSICAL EDUCATION ACTIVITIES

Spatial awareness is the ability to make decisions about an object's positional changes in space. In short it is the awareness of three-dimensional space position changes.

Developing spatial awareness requires two sequential phases:
1) Identifying the location of objects in relation to one's own body in space, and
2) Locating more than one object in relation to each object and independent of one's own body.

Spatial awareness can be increased with the help of certain activities. An example would be activities using different sized balls, boxes, or hoops. You can have the children move towards and away, under and over, in front of and behind, and inside, outside, and beside the objects.

CONCEPT OF BODY AWARENESS APPLIED TO PHYSICAL EDUCATION ACTIVITIES

Body awareness is a person's understanding of his or her own body parts and the capability of their movements.

Instructors can assess body awareness by watching students play a game of "Simon Says" and asking the students to touch different body parts. You can also instruct students to form their bodies into various shapes, such as, from straight to round to twisted and to fit into different sized spaces.

In addition, you can instruct children to touch one part of their body with another. Also they could be asked to use the various body parts such as to stamp their feet, twist their neck, clap their hands, nod their heads, wiggle their noses, snap their fingers, open their mouths, shrug their shoulders, bend their knees, close their eyes, bend their elbows, or wiggle their toes.

CONCEPT OF EFFORT QUALITIES APPLIED TO PHYSICAL EDUCATION

Effort qualities are the qualities of movement that apply the mechanical principles of balance, time, and force.

Balance - Activities for balance include having children move on their hands and feet, lean, move on lines, and balance and hold shapes while moving.

Time - Activities using the concept of time can include having children move as fast as they can and as slow as they can in specified, timed movement patterns.

Force - Activities using the concept of force can include having students use their bodies to produce enough force to move them through space. They can also paddle balls against walls and jump over objects of various heights.

SKILL 1.2 **Growth and motor development: role of perception in motor development, such as in spatial movement relationships; neurophysiology of motor control; effects of maturation and experience on motor patterns; biological and environmental influences on gender differences in motor performances**

PERCEPTION AND SPATIAL AWARENESS IN MOTOR CONTROL

See Skill 1.1

NEUROPHYSIOLOGY OF MOTOR CONTROL

The nervous system plays a vital role in motor control. It allows for effective use of the skeletal muscles and coordinates with the brain, skeleton, and joints.

Before looking at the function of the nervous system, we must first examine the basic anatomy. First, a muscle consists of a group of muscle fibers. At least one motor nerve, which consists of fibrous extensions (axons) of a group of motor neurons, controls every muscle fiber in the body. As axons enter the muscles, they branch off into terminals forming a neuromuscular junction with a single muscle fiber. A motor neuron together with the muscle fibers it supplies is known as a motor unit.

Muscular contraction occurs when a motor neuron transmits an electrical impulse. The number of muscle fibers per motor unit varies between four and several hundreds. The muscles controlling very fine movements (e.g. fingers and eyes) have very small motor units. Examples of movements controlled by small motor units include writing, sewing, and tying shoelaces. These types of motor skills generally are not present in the early stages of life. Larger muscles (e.g. hips, legs) controlling less precise movements have large motor units. Examples of such movements include walking, throwing objects, and performing sit-ups. These movements are present even in the earliest stages of life.

Proper development and function of the nervous system does not always occur. Improper development results in various diseases that affect motor control including cerebral palsy, dyspraxia, multiple sclerosis, and Parkinson's disease.

RELATIONSHIP BETWEEN HUMAN GROWTH AND DEVELOPMENT AND APPROPRIATE PHYSICAL ACTIVITY

Understanding the rate of the developmental growth process that occurs during adolescence will help educators understand growth and development norms. It will help them identify early or late maturing students. The age when the puberty growth spurt occurs and the speed with which adolescents experience puberty vary greatly within each gender. It may affect participation in physical activity and sports. If the instructor pays attention to the varying body sizes and maturity stages, forming teams in co-educational classes can easily accommodate the needs of both genders' changing maturities. Starting in middle school and continuing into high school, it is perfectly acceptable for boys and girls to participate in non-contact physical activities together. These activities rely on lower-body strength and agility (e.g. capture the flag, ultimate Frisbee, running). In more physical activities that require upper body strength, coaches should form teams based on individual skill levels to prevent injury. Matching teams evenly based on skill and maturity is important. This ensures that individual skill level deficiencies are not as apparent and the activity remains fun for all participants. Teachers need to monitor and adjust physical activities as required to ensure a positive, competitive experience. Appropriate activities would include individual or partner badminton or tennis matches and team competitions such as flag football.

BIOLOGICAL AND ENVIRONMENTAL INFLUENCES ON GENDER DIFFERENCES IN MOTOR PERFORMANCES

The differences between males and females in motor performance result from certain biological and environmental influences. Generally, people perceive the males as stronger, faster, and more active than females. This higher activity level can stem from childhood behaviors influenced by certain environmental factors. The superior motor performance results largely from the biological make up of males versus females.

In most cases, the male body contains less fat mass and more muscle mass than the female body. In addition, the type of muscle differs between males and females. Males have more fast-twitch muscle fibers allowing for more short duration, high intensity movements such as jumping and sprinting. In addition, males generally, but not always, display better coordination. Females have proved their superiority at certain activities, such as skipping. They also tend to display better fine movements, such as neater handwriting.

Certain environmental factors also contribute to the gender differences in motor performance. As children, boys tend to be more physically active. Society expects boys to participate in sports and play games that involve running around, such as tag and foot races. On the other hand, society expects girls to be more social and less active. They participate in activities such as playing with dolls. In addition, parents rarely ask girls to perform tasks involving manual labor.

While these sedentary tasks have value, it is important for both males and females to participate in adequate amount of physical activity each day. If children develop this type of active lifestyle early in life, they are more likely to maintain it throughout adulthood.

SKILL 1.3 **Motor learning: classical and current theories of motor learning, variables that affect learning and performance, effects of individual differences**

Effective physical education supports psychomotor, cognitive, and affective development.

Physical education through the Psychomotor Domain contributes to movement skills as a participant and spectator in sports and other physical activities; contributes skills to utilize leisure hours in mental and cultural pursuits; contributes skills necessary to the preservation of the natural environment.

Physical education in the Cognitive Domain contributes to academic achievement; is related to higher thought processes via motor activity; contributes to knowledge of exercise, health and disease; contributes to an understanding of the human body; contributes to an understanding of the role of physical activity and sport in the American culture; and contributes to the knowledgeable consumption of goods and services.

Physical education in the Affective Domain contributes to self-actualization, self-esteem, and a healthy response to physical activity; contributes to an appreciation of beauty; contributes to directing one's life toward worthy goals; emphasizes humanism; affords individuals the chance to enjoy rich social experiences through play; assists cooperative play with others; teaches courtesy, fair play, and good sportsmanship; contributes to humanitarianism.

Teaching methods to facilitate psychomotor learning include:

1. **Task/Reciprocal** - The instructor integrates task learning into the learning set up by utilizing stations.

2. **Command/Direct** - Task instruction is teacher-centered. The teacher clearly explains the goals, explains and demonstrates the skills, allocates time for practice, and frequently monitors student progress.

3. **Contingency/Contract** - A style of task instruction that rewards completion of tasks.

Techniques that facilitate psychomotor learning include:

1. **Reflex movements** - Activities that create an automatic response to some stimuli. Responses include flexing, extending, stretching, and postural adjustment.

2. **Basic fundamental locomotor movements** - Activities that utilize instinctive patterns of movement established by combining reflex movements.

3. **Perceptual abilities** - Activities that involve interpreting auditory, visual, tactile stimuli in order to coordinate adjustments.

4. **Physical abilities** - Activities to develop physical characteristics of fitness providing students with the stamina necessary for highly advanced, skilled movement.

5. **Skilled movements** - Activities that involve instinctive, effective performance of complex movement including vertical and horizontal components.

6. **Nondiscursive communication** - Activities necessitating expression as part of the movement.

Teaching methods that facilitate cognitive learning include:

1. **Problem Solving** - The instructor presents the initial task and students come to an acceptable solution in unique and divergent ways.

2. **Conceptual Theory** - The instructor's focus is on acquisition of knowledge.

3. **Guided Inquiry** – Stages of instructions strategically guide students through a sequence of experiences.

Initially, performance of skills will be variable, inconsistent, error-prone, "off-time," and awkward. Students' focus will be on remembering what to do. Instructors should emphasize clear information regarding the skill's biomechanics. They should correct errors in gross movement that effect significant parts of the skill. To prevent students from being overburdened with too much information, they should only perform one or two elements at a time. Motivation results from supportive and encouraging comments. Peer to peer encouragement is also very useful and helpful.

Techniques to facilitate cognitive learning include:

1. **Transfer of learning** – Identifying similar movements of a previously learned skill in a new skill.

2. **Planning for slightly longer instructions and demonstrations** as students memorize cues and skills.

3. **Using appropriate language** according to the level of each student.

4. **Conceptual Thinking** - giving students who are more capable more responsibility for their learning.

Aids to facilitate cognitive learning include:

1. Frequent assessments of student performance

2. Movement activities incorporating principles of biomechanics

3. Laser discs, computers and software

4. Video recordings of student performance

FACTORS AFFECTING THE LEARNING ENVIRONMENT

Individual characteristics of students including age, gender, coordination level, physical ability, and fitness level greatly affect the learning environment. Physical education instructors must recognize these individual differences and adapt the learning environment to meet the needs of a diverse student population.

COMPETENCY 2.0 MOVEMENT FORMS

SKILL 2.1 Dance and rhythmic activities: dance forms and dance skill analysis

Students of dance acquire many skills during their course of study. The student identifies and demonstrates movement elements in a dance performance. He/she uses correct body alignment, strength, flexibility, and stamina (for more demanding performances). Crucial to any form of dance is the concept of coordination in the performance of technical movements. Technical movements must look as though they are easy to perform. The dancer must perform technical dance skills with artistic expression along with musicality and rhythm. As the student progresses, he or she will perform extended movement sequences and rhythmic patterns. The student will then have enough experience to introduce his or her own stylistic nuance into the performance. The student will also be able to improvise to solve movement problems. He or she will learn to make choices based on the movement responses of other dancers in the ensemble. Through continued experience, he or she will become a skillful, seasoned dancer whose technique and ability will transcend any form of dance.

Instructors can create rhythmic activities by putting on music with a strong beat and asking students to dance to the beat. Tell the students to listen to the beat and move accordingly (e.g. stomping their feet or clapping their hands in time with the beat). It's important for children to learn to move to various sounds and use their bodies to mimic the beat. Another idea is to have the students take turns beating on a coffee can while trying to keep movements in synchronization with the rhythm. In more structured dance forms, technique or skill comes into play. For instance, in ballet, dancers must have good flexibility, body control, and coordination. Ballet dancers must also have a sense of rhythm, an understanding of music, good turnout and alignment, and a sense of balance and counterbalance. These skills take many years to acquire. Once they are acquired it takes many more years to master and maintain. Ballet dancing may express a mood, tell a story, or simply reflect a piece of music. It is the most classical of all dance forms. Other types of music may have similar requirements in terms of sense of musicality and rhythm. For example, tap dance requires a greater degree of footwork. Modern dance is comparable to ballet, but is more flowing and less rigid.

DANCE CONCEPTS, FORMS, AND BASIC VOCABULARY – JAZZ AND BALLET

There are several forms of dance including modern, ballet, jazz, country, ballroom, and hip-hop. Though essentially very different from each other, they all have similarities. A sense of musicality is the one common requirement for each of the dance forms. Along with that, timing, coordination, flexibility, and an interest in the concept of dance itself is essential.

We all know that we will probably experience greater success when we engage in activities that we are interested in and enjoy. Understanding of most dance forms requires knowledge of basic vocabulary. Examples for some specific words are turns or kick ball turns in jazz; the shuffle or the flap in tap dance. Ballet has more specialized vocabulary than any other dance form. For example, plie, to bend; tendu, to stretch; degage, to disengage; fouette, to whip; fondu, to melt; ronde jambe, circle of the leg; pirouette, to turn on one leg; port de bras, movement of the arms; and assemble, to assemble.

Integral to dance and particularly ballet are the concepts of balance and counterbalance, pull-up and turnout, weight distribution and alignment, including shoulders down, hips square, legs turned out, and chest lifted.

In ballet, there are many different dance forms and techniques that a dancer can follow. Three of the larger ones are the Cecchetti, Russian Vaganova, and Royal Academy of Dance, (RAD), programs. They all have different levels for the dancers starting from the beginner to the advanced. Each of the dance form has its set of advantages and disadvantages. The Cecchetti Society developed the Cecchetti technique from the teachings of the great ballet master Enrico Cecchetti. It is a full syllabus designed to train dancers for professional work. One notable emphasis in the Cecchetti syllabus is that the arms flow and blend from position to position more than any other technique. The Cecchetti technique is the core of the program at the National Ballet School of Canada. The Russian Vaganova technique is named after and derived from the teachings of Agrippina Vaganova, who was the artistic director of the Kirov Ballet for many years. In the Vaganova method, the dancers bring attention to their hands. The hands do not flow invisibly from one position to the next, as in the Cecchetti method. In the Vaganova ballet form the hands are left behind and turn at the last moment. This is how the "flapping" look, that many dancers make with their hands, is created. In the Vaganova method, the exercises for each level are not formally established as in the RAD method. Each teacher choreographs his own class according to specialized guidelines and the students dance that class in their examinations. The Vaganova method forms the core of the program at the Royal Winnipeg Ballet School. The RAD syllabus is very common. It is well suited to dance classes in community dance schools where the students usually do no more than an average of one class per day. If you go to the ballet school in your community, there is a good chance you will be taught using the RAD method. The American School of Ballet teaches the Balanchine method. Created by George Balanchine in the American School of Ballet, the Balanchine method allows dancers to dance Balanchine's choreography much more easily than other dancers can. In the Balanchine method the hands are held differently again from any of the other forms.

DANCE CONCEPTS, FORMS, AND BASIC VOCABULARY – FOLK AND TAP

Folk dance is a term used to describe a large number of dances that originated in Europe and share several common characteristics. Most folk dances practiced today were created before the 20th century. They were practiced by people with little or no training. For this reason, folk dances are usually characterized by a spontaneous style, adaptable movements, and culturally distinctive steps representative of the dance's country of origin. Types of folk dancing include the contra dance, English country-dance, and Maypole dance.

Contra dance is a term used to describe folk dances in which couples dance in two facing lines. A pair of such lines is a set, and these sets are generally arranged to run the length of a long hall. The head of a set is at the end of the line closest to the band and is the caller. At contra dance events dancers perform several different folk dances. The caller or dance leader teaches the movements of a dance to the dancers during the "walk through". A walk through is a short period of time before the next type of dance begins. During the walk through, all dancers mark the movements following the caller's instructions. At contra dance events in North America, contra dancers traditionally change partners for every dance, while in the United Kingdom, dancers remain with the same partner for the entire evening.

Square dance refers to a type of folk dance in which four couples begin and end each sequence in a square formation. When four couples align themselves in such a manner, the formation is called "sets-in-order," and dances that use such formations are historically known as "quadrille." Similar to folk dance, American square dance steps are based on traditional European dances. At every square dance event, the dance caller prompts participants through a sequence of steps to the beat throughout the entirety of each dance. The caller does not usually participate in the dancing. Steps common to many square dances include allemande left and allemande right, where couples face, take hands, and circle around one another; promenade, where partners cross hands and walk to a counter-clockwise position; and circle right and circle left, where all dancers grasp hands and move round in a circle. Traditionally, the caller explains the steps in each square dance at the beginning of a session.

Tap is a form of dance born in the United States during the 19th century in which the dancer sounds out the rhythm by clicking taps on the toes and heels of his shoes. This form of percussive music and dance is believed to have evolved from a fusion of Irish and African Shuffle in New York City during the 1830s. One common characteristic of modern tap dance is "syncopation," where choreographies generally begin on the eighth music beat. Learning to tap dance is a cumulative process in which new information builds on previously learned steps and terms.

To teach tap dance successfully, instructors must first teach simple steps that make up the foundation of tap before introducing complex movements. The most basic steps of tap include the walk, step, heel, step-heel, stamp, ball-change, brush, toe tap, shuffle, side shuffle, back shuffle, and cramp roll. Dance instructors can combine these steps to form simple routines for beginners. Once students have mastered these steps, dancers can move on to attempt movements such as the buffalo, Maxi Ford, Cincinnati, pullback, wings, toe clips, and riffs.

DANCE AEROBICS

Dance aerobics is any type of cardiovascular exercise that is put to music, ranging from country line dancing to hip-hop. Aerobic dance can be performed on three different levels. High-impact aerobics include movements such as jumping which cause both feet to lose contact with the ground simultaneously. In low-impact aerobics one foot remains in contact with the ground at all times the third level is the step aerobics, in which dancers move on and around a slightly raised platform. A beneficial aerobics session is composed of three stages. During the warm-up, which usually lasts for 5-10 minutes, slow movements such as walking in place and stretching will prepare participants for more vigorous activity. The high-impact stage of dance aerobics follows the warm-up. High impact should last 20-30 minutes, and include anything from a dance routine to a step class. Moves common to many dance aerobic classes include the grapevine combined with kicks and lunges, high kicks, jumping jacks, and forward and back double kicks. Step routines are generally composed of movements on and off a platform, and also include kicks, swats, and lunges. In between movements of the high-impact period, dancers should always maintain constant movement, walking or marching in place. This will help keep up their heart rate and burn more calories. The last 5-10 minutes of a dance aerobics session should be a cool down period, during which participants again stretch all muscles and slowly lower their heart rate.

SKILL 2.2 Gymnastics: stunts and tumbling, use of gymnastic apparatus, movement themes in educational games

GYMNASTIC MOVEMENTS – STUNTS, TUMBLING, APPARATUS WORK, AND FLOOR EXERCISE

SAFETY PRACTICES

Gymnastics, especially at the advanced level, leaves little room for error to avoid possible serious injury. To avoid injuries from falls, instructors, coaches, and other participants should act as spotters during complex aerial stunts. In addition, proper stretching and strength training is necessary to help prevent muscular and skeletal injuries. Instructors must not require or allow students to perform stunts that are beyond their limitations or abilities.

Additionally, proper equipment, such as mats, landing pads, pulleys, balance beams and bars must be in good condition and checked daily for any lose cables, screws or damage of any kind. Any equipment that is not in good and safe condition for any reason should not be used until it is fixed or replaced.

Basic Movement Patterns	Movement Variables
- Landings - Locomotions - Statics - Rotations - Swings - Springs	- Body - Space - Effort - Relationships

Tumbling and gymnastics are two specialized skills within the physical education curriculum. To assess competency in tumbling and gymnastics, physical education instructors generally ask students to perform various tumbling and gymnastics movements. They should ask the students to perform simple movements in the beginning and progress to more complex movements as the students' skills develop. By practicing tumbling and gymnastics, a student's movement activity skills will improve. By assessing these skills, teachers will gain insight of the student's ability at gymnastics and tumbling activities.

Balance tests – Bass Test of Dynamic Balance (lengthwise and crosswise), Johnson Modification of the Bass Test of Dynamic Balance, modified sideward leap, and balance beam walk.

Proper stretching and strength building exercises are necessary for gymnastics. A useful, brief warm-up can consist of push-ups, sit-ups, and flexibility exercises for hamstrings, back, ankles, neck, wrists, and shoulders. An aerial is one example of a stunt (i.e. difficult physical feat) in which the gymnast turns completely over in the air without touching the apparatus with his or her hands. Floor exercise and tumbling can include somersault, backward and forward rolls, cartwheels, forward straddle roll, back tuck, back handsprings, handstand, etc. Apparatus work is done on the vaulting horse, balance beam, and uneven bars. A strong run, dynamism, power, and precision in the rotations are characteristics of an efficient vault. The main characteristics for the beam are a well-developed sense of balance and great power of concentration. The uneven bars demand strength as well as concentration, courage, coordination, precision, and split-second timing.

RHYTHMIC GYMNASTICS AND EDUCATIONAL GYMNASTICS

Rhythmic gymnastics is a sport, which combines dance and gymnastics with the use of balls, hoops, ribbons, ropes, and clubs. Gymnasts perform on a carpet to music either individually or in a group of five. In competition, gymnasts perform leaps, pivots, balances, and other elements to demonstrate flexibility and coordination. The gymnast must completely integrate the apparatus into the routine and perform specific moves with each apparatus. Individual routines last from 1 minute and 15 seconds to 1 minute and 30 seconds, while group routines last from 2 minutes 15 seconds to 2 minutes and 30 seconds. The main difference between rhythmic and artistic gymnastics is that acrobatic skill is not allowed in the former. In fact, a gymnast is penalized for incorporating acrobatic skill into his routine. However, pre-acrobatic elements such as forward and backward shoulder rolls, fish-flops, and tah-dahs are permitted. In addition, the new Code of Points permits walkovers and cartwheels. Originality and risk are integral parts of this sport, and no two routines are ever the same.

In educational gymnastics, students learn to use and manage their bodies in safe, efficient and creative ways. Educational gymnastics can utilize certain fixed equipment such as mats, bars, ropes, and boxes. It is also known as "body management" because the activities provide opportunities for students to learn to manage their own bodies. Instead of a series of gymnastics stunts, they select, refine and perform the six Basic Movement Patterns of Landings, Locomotions, Statics, Rotations, Swings, and Springs in a variety of contexts and environments. Emphasis is on challenges and problem solving. Instructors use the movement variables of body, space, effort, and relationships to design movement learning experiences. Students work individually, in pairs, and in groups to create movement sequences and structures.

Elaborate facilities are not required in this approach. In fact, many good educational gymnastics programs take place out-of-doors in natural settings. While large-scale gymnastics equipment is not essential for providing students with quality movement learning experiences, such equipment is certainly advantageous. Another advantage of educational gymnastics is that it provides for the development of the upper body. It is much easier and more common to develop strength in the lower body than in the upper body. Many everyday events such as walking, running and jumping enhance lower body strength. Most team games and sports emphasize lower body strength and tend to neglect upper body development. Gymnastics also helps to build overall muscular strength and flexibility. There is also equal development of both left and right sides of the body because most gymnastics activities involve simultaneous use of both arms (e.g. rolls, hangs, swings, supports) or both legs (e.g. springs, tumbling). In contrast, many game activities that involve the use of an implement (e.g., bat, racquet, stick) or object (e.g., beanbag, ball, Frisbee) tend to favor the development of one side of the body more than the other.

Finally, if educational gymnastics experiences are to be truly "educational," then we must ask in what ways are they educational? In short, these experiences are educational because they start with the needs of students. The instructor presents the students with movement problems, which the students must solve, asks questions to gain the cognitive involvement of students, offers various solutions in the form of movement sequences, and guides students to reflect upon and synthesize their experiences. Students gain knowledge and understanding of the mechanical principles associated with the Basic Movement Patterns of gymnastics. This increases their ability to apply these principles.

SKILL 2.3 Games: game forms, including invasion games; cooperative and competitive games; analysis of skills, rules, and strategies of particular games.

INVASION GAMES

Invasion games are a class of games that involve a player or team penetrating the territory of the opponent in an attempt to score points by shooting, throwing, kicking, or striking an object or ball into the opponent's goal. Common invasion games in the physical education setting include basketball, soccer, flag football, lacrosse, and hockey. We discuss rules, strategies, and sport-specific skills in

COOPERATIVE AND COMPETITIVE GAMES

Cooperative games are a class of games that promote teamwork and social interaction. The emphasis is on activity, fitness, skill development, and cooperation, rather than competition. There are many cooperative games available to the physical education instructor that helps develop various coordination skills and teamwork. Examples of cooperative games include throwing and catching, freeze tag, water tag and parachute.

Water fitness activities and games should place emphasis on generating a lot of movement in the pool (gross motor activities). They also may incorporate activities that require more coordinated manipulations, like catching a ball (fine motor). Sample games include:

- **Water Tag** – Children can attempt to catch each other in the pool. When someone is caught, he becomes 'it'. Variations include freeze tag (where a caught student isn't allowed to move until someone swims between their legs to free them) and base tag (where some sections of the pool, for example the ladders or the walls, are a safe 'base'. Rules must be in place limiting the time that a student can spend on the base). Water tag emphasizes gross motor activities. Safety issue: students may not hold other students or grab other students in the water.

- **Water Dodgeball** – Students divide into two teams, one on either side of the pool. They play dodgeball, throwing a ball from one side to the other. A student who is hit by the ball is captured by the opposing team, but if the ball is caught, the thrower is captured instead. Safety issue: students may not throw the ball at another student's head at close range.

-
- **Relay Races** – Students divide into teams and perform relay races (i.e. one student swims the length of the pool and back. When he returns the next student in the team does the same. This is repeated until the whole team has completed the task). This can incorporate various swimming strokes; either all team members use the same stroke or each team member uses a different stroke.

Competitive games are a class of games that emphasize score, winning, and beating an opponent. Physical education instructors should integrate competitive games into the curriculum to generate student interest and teach concepts of fair play and sportsmanship. Competitive games are most suitable for students that are more mature and possess more developed skills. All traditional sporting events are competitive games.

SKILL 2.4 **Individual/dual/team sports: analysis of skills, injury prevention and safety, rules and strategies, facilities and equipment, lifetime activities and recreational pursuits, adventure and outdoor pursuits, and the martial arts.**

RULES OF PLAY, STRATEGIES AND TERMINOLOGY

ARCHERY:

- Arrows that bounce off the target or go through the target count as 7 points.

- Arrows landing on lines between two rings receive the higher score of the two rings.

- Arrows hitting the petticoat receive no score.

BADMINTON:

- Intentionally balking an opponent or making preliminary feints results in a fault (side in = loss of serve; side out = point awarded to side in).

- When a shuttlecock falls on a line, it is in play (i.e. a fair play).

- If the striking team hits shuttlecock before it crosses net it is a fault.

- Touching the net when the shuttlecock is in play is a fault.
- The same player hitting the shuttlecock twice is a fault.
- The shuttlecock going through the net is a fault.

BASKETBALL:

- A player touching the floor on or outside the boundary line is out-of-bounds.
- The ball is out of bounds if it touches anything (a player, the floor, an object, or any person) that is on or outside the boundary line.
- An offensive player remaining in the three-second zone of the free-throw lane for more than three seconds is a violation.
- A ball firmly held by two opposing players results in a jump ball.
- A throw-in is awarded to the opposing team of the last player touching a ball that goes out-of-bounds.

BOWLING:

- No score for a pin knocked down by a pinsetter (human or mechanical).
- There is no score for the pins when any part of the foot, hand, or arm extends or crosses over the foul line (even after ball leaves the hand). If any part of the body contacts division boards, walls, or uprights that are beyond the foul line again there is no score.
- There is no count for pins displaced or knocked down by a ball leaving the lane before it reaches the pins.
- There is no count when balls rebound from the rear cushion.

RACQUETBALL/HANDBALL:

- A server stepping outside service area when serving faults.
- The server is out (relinquishes serve) if he/she steps outside the serving zone twice in succession while serving.
- Server is out if he/she fails to hit the ball rebounding off the floor during the serve.
- The opponent must have a chance to take a position or the referee must call for play before the server can serve the ball.

- The ball is re-served if the receiver is not behind the short line when the ball is served.

- A served ball that hits the front line and does not land behind the short line is "short"; therefore, it is a fault. The ball is also short when it hits the front wall and two sidewalls before it lands on the floor behind the short line.

- A serve is a fault when the ball touches the ceiling from rebounding off the front wall.

- A fault occurs when any part of the foot steps over the outer edges of the service or the short line while serving.

- A hinder (dead ball) is called when a returned ball hits an opponent on its way to the front wall - even if the ball continues to the front wall.

- A hinder is any intentional or unintentional interference to an opponent's opportunity to return the ball.

SOCCER:

The following are direct free-kick offenses:

- Hand or arm contact with the ball
- Using hands to hold an opponent
- Pushing an opponent
- Striking/kicking/tripping or attempting to strike/kick/trip an opponent
- Goalie using the ball to strike an opponent
- Jumping at or charging an opponent
- Kneeing an opponent
- Any contact fouls

The following are indirect free-kick offenses:

- Same player playing the ball twice at the kickoff, on a throw-in, on a goal kick, on a free kick, or on a corner kick.

- The goalie delaying the game by holding the ball or carrying the ball more than four steps.

- Failure to notify the referee of substitutions/re-substitutions and that player then handling the ball in the penalty area.

- Any person who is not a player entering playing field without a referee's permission.

- Unsportsmanlike actions or words in reference to a referee's decision.

- Dangerously lowering the head or raising the foot too high to make a play.

- A player resuming play after being ordered off the field.

- Offsides – an offensive player must have two defenders between him and the goal when a teammate passes the ball to him or else he is offside.

- Attempting to kick the ball when the goalkeeper has possession or interference with the goalkeeper to hinder him/her from releasing the ball.

- Illegal charging.

- Leaving the playing field without referee's permission while the ball is in play.

SOFTBALL:

- Each team plays nine players in the field (sometimes 10 for slow pitch).

- Field positions are one pitcher, one catcher, four infielders, and three outfielders (four outfielders in ten player formats).

- The four bases are 60 feet apart.

- Any ball hit outside of the first or third base line is a foul ball (i.e. runners cannot advance and the pitch counts as a strike against the batter)

- If a batter receives three strikes (i.e. failed attempts at hitting the ball) in a single at bat he/she strikes out.

- The pitcher must start with both feet on the pitcher's rubber and can only take one step forward when delivering the underhand pitch.

- A base runner is out if:

    - A. The opposition tags him with the ball before he reaches a base.
    - B. The ball reaches first base before he does.
    - C. He runs outside the base path to avoid a tag.
    - D. A batted ball strikes him in fair territory.

- A team must maintain the same batting order throughout the game.
- Runners cannot lead off and base stealing is illegal.
- Runners may overrun first base, but can be tagged out if off any other base.

TENNIS:

A player loses a point when:

- The ball bounces twice on her side of the net.
- The player returns the ball to any place outside the designated areas.
- The player stops or touches the ball in the air before it lands out-of-bounds.
- The player intentionally strikes the ball twice with the racket.
- The ball strikes any part of a player or racket after initial attempt to hit the ball.
- A player reaches over the net to hit the ball.
- A player throws his racket at the ball.
- The ball strikes any permanent fixture that is out-of-bounds (other than the net).
    - a ball touching the net and landing inside the boundary lines is in play (except on the serve, where a ball contacting the net results in a "let" – replay of the point)
- A player fails, on two consecutive attempts, to serve the ball into the designated area (i.e. double fault).

TRACK AND FIELD:

The following are common track and field events:

- Sprint Races – 100, 200, 400 meter dash; 110, 400 meter hurdles
- Distance Races – one-mile, 5000 and 10000 meter foot races
- Jumping Events – high jump, long jump, broad jump, triple jump, pole vault
- Relay Races – team sprint or distance foot races
- Throwing Events – hammer, discus, javelin, shot put

Rules of track and field events:
- In all sprint races, runners must stay in their lane on the track and the first person to cross the finish line wins.
    - depending on local rules, one or two "false starts" – running before the start signal – results in disqualification
- In all jumping events, participants must take off on or before a designated "foul line" and the person with the longest jump wins.
    - "foul" jumps do not receive a score
- In all relay races, teams must pass a baton within a designated transition area and the first team to cross the finish line with the baton wins.
    - failed exchanges result in disqualification
- In all throwing events, participants must release the object within a specified area and the person with the longest throw wins.
    - releasing the object outside the designated area is a "foul" and foul throws do not receive a measurement

VOLLEYBALL:

The following infractions by the receiving team result in a point awarded to the serving side and an infraction by the serving team results in side-out:

- Illegal serves or serving out of turn.

- Illegal returns or catching or holding the ball.

- Dribbling or a player touching the ball twice in succession.

- Contact with the net (two opposing players making contact with the net at the same time results in a replay of the point).

- Touching the ball after it has been played three times without passing over the net.

- A player's foot completely touching the floor over the centerline.

- Reaching under the net and touching a player or the ball while the ball is in play.

- The players changing positions prior to the serve.

APPROPRIATE STRATEGIES FOR GAME AND SPORT SITUATIONS

ARCHERY STRATEGIES FOR CORRECTING ERRORS IN AIMING AND RELEASING:

- Shifting position.
- Relaxing both the arms and shoulders at the moment of release.
- Reaching point of aim before releasing string.
- Pointing aim to the right or left of direct line between the archer and the target's center.
- Aiming with the left eye.
- Sighting with both eyes.
- Using the proper arrow.

BADMINTON STRATEGIES:

Strategies for Return of Service

- Returning serves with shots that are straight ahead.
- Returning service so that the opponent must move out of his/her starting position.
- Returning long serves with an overhead clear or drop shot to near corner.
- Returning short serves with underhand clear or a net drop to near corner.

Strategies for Serving

- Serving long to the backcourt near centerline.
- Serving short when opponent is standing too deep in his/her receiving court to return the serve. Using a short serve to eliminate a smash return if opponent has a powerful smash from the backcourt.

BASKETBALL STRATEGIES:

Use a Zone Defense

- To prevent drive-ins for easy lay-up shots.
- When playing area is small.

- When team is in foul trouble.
- To keep an excellent rebounder near opponent's basket.
- When opponents' outside shooting is weak.
- When opponents have an advantage in height.
- When opponents have an exceptional offensive player, or when the best defenders cannot handle one-on-one defense.

Offensive Strategies against Zone Defense

- Using quick, sharp passes to penetrate zone, forcing opposing player out of assigned position.
- Overloading and mismatching.

Offensive Strategies for One-On-One Defense

- Using the "pick-and-roll" and the "give-and-go" to screen defensive players so as to open up offensive players for shot attempts.
- Teams may use free-lancing (spontaneous one-one-one offense), but more commonly they use "sets" of plays.

BOWLING FOR SPARES STRATEGIES:

- Identifying the key pin and determining where it must be hit to pick up remaining pins.
- Using the three basic alignments: center position for center pins, left position for left pins, and right position for right pins.
- Rolling the spare ball in the same manner as rolled for the first ball of frame.
- Concentrating harder for spare ball because of the reduced opportunity for pin action and margin of error.

HANDBALL OR RACQUETBALL STRATEGIES:

- Identifying opponent's strengths and weaknesses.
- Making opponent use the less dominant hand or the backhand shots if they are weaker.

- Frequently alternating fastballs and lobs to change the pace (changing the pace is particularly effective for serving).

- Maintaining position near middle of court (the well) that is close enough to play low balls and corner shots.

- Placing shots that keep opponent's position at a disadvantage to return cross-court and angle shots.

- Using high lob shots that go overhead but do not hit the back wall with enough force to rebound. This will drive an opponent out of position when he/she persistently plays close to the front wall.

SOCCER STRATEGIES:

- **Heading** – using the head to pass, to shoot, or to clear the ball.

- **Tackling** – objective is to take possession of the ball from an opponent. Successful play requires knowledgeable utilization of space.

TENNIS STRATEGIES:

- Lobbing – using a high, lob shot for defense giving the player more time to get back into position.

- Identifying opponent's weaknesses and attacking them. Recognizing and protecting one's own weaknesses.

- Outrunning and out-thinking an opponent.

- Using change of pace, lobs, spins, approaching the net, and deception at the correct time.

- Hitting cross-court (from corner to corner of the court) for maximum safety and opportunity to regain position.

- Directing the ball not towards the opponent.

VOLLEYBALL STRATEGIES:

- Using forearm passes (bumps, digs, or passes) to play balls below the waist, to play balls that are driven hard, to pass the serve, and to contact balls distant from a player.

TERMINOLOGY OF VARIOUS PHYSICAL EDUCATION ACTIVITIES

ARCHERY TERMINOLOGY:

- Addressing the target – standing ready to shoot with a proper shooting stance.

- Anchor point – specific location on the archer's face to which index finger comes while holding and aiming.

- Archery golf (adaptation of golf to archery) – players shoot for holes, scoring according to the number of shots required to hit the target.

- Arm guard – a piece of leather or plastic worn on the inside of the forearm, protecting the arm from the bowstring.

- Arrow plate – a protective piece of hard material set into the bow where the arrow crosses it.

- Arrow rest – a small projection at the top of the bow handle where the arrow rests.

- Back – the side of the bow away from the shooter.

- Bow arm – the arm that holds the bow.

- Bow sight – a device attached to the bow through which the archer sights when aiming.

- Bow weight – designates the amount of effort needed to pull a bowstring to a specific distance.

- Cant – shooting while holding the bow slightly turned or tilted.

- Cast – the distance a bow can shoot an arrow.

- Clout shooting – a type of shooting using a target 48 feet in diameter laid on the ground at a distance of 180 yards for men and 120 or 140 yards for women. Participants usually shoot 36 arrows per round.

- Cock/Index feather – the feather that is set at a right angle to the arrow nock; differently colored than the other two feathers.

- Creeping – letting the drawing hand move forward at the release.

- Crest – the archer's identifying marks located just below the fletchings.

- Draw – pulling the bowstring back into the anchor position.

- End – a specific number of arrows shot at one time or from one position before retrieval of arrows.

- Face – the part of the bow facing the shooter.

- Finger tab – a leather flap worn on the drawing hand protecting the fingers and providing a smooth release of the bowstring.

- Fletchings – the feathers of the arrow that give guidance to its flight.

- Flight shooting – shooting an arrow the farthest possible distance.

- Handle – the grip at the midsection of the bow.

- Hen feathers – the two feathers that are not set at right angles to the arrow nock.

- Instinctive shooting – aiming and shooting instinctively rather than using a bow sight or point-of-aim method.

- Limbs – upper and lower parts of the bow divided by the handle.

- Nock – the groove in the arrow's end where the string is placed.

- Nocking point – the point on the string where the arrow is placed.

- Notch – the grooves of the upper and lower tips of the limbs where the bowstring is fitted.

- Over bow – using too strong a bow that is too powerful to pull a bowstring the proper distance.

- Overdraw – drawing the bow so that the pile of the arrow is inside the bow.

- Petticoat – the part of the target face outside the white ring.

- Pile/point – the arrow's pointed, metal tip.

- Plucking – jerking the drawing hand laterally away from the face on the release causing the arrow's flight to veer to the left.

- Point-blank range – the distance from the target where the point of aim is right on the bull's eye.

- Point-of-aim – a method of aiming that aligns the pile of arrow with the target.

- Quiver – a receptacle for carrying or holding arrows.

- Recurve bow – a bow that is curved on the ends.

- Release – the act of letting the bowstring slip off the fingertips.

- Round – the term used to indicate shooting a specified number of arrows at a designated distance or distances.

- Roving – an outdoor archery game that uses natural targets (trees, bushes, stumps, etc.) for competition.

- Serving – the thread wrapped around the bowstring at the nocking point.

- Shaft – the long, body part of the arrow.

- Spine – the rigidity and flexibility characteristics of an arrow.

- Tackle – archery equipment referred to in its entirety.

- Target face – the painted front of a target.

- Trajectory – the flight path of the arrow.

- Vane – an arrow's plastic feather.

BADMINTON TERMINOLOGY:

- Alley – the area on each side of the court used for doubles that is 1.5 feet wide.

- Around-the-head stroke – an overhead stroke used to hit a forehand-like overhead stroke that is on the backhand side of the body.

- Back alley – the area between the baseline and the doubles long service line.

- Backcourt – the back third of the court.

- Backhand – a stroke made on the non-racket side of the body.

- Baseline – the back boundary line of the court.

- Bird – another name for the shuttlecock/shuttle.

- Block – a soft shot used mainly to defend a smash; intercepting opponent's smash and returning it back over the net.

- Carry/Throw – a call when the shuttle remains on the racket during a stroke. It is legal if the racket follows the intended line of flight.

- Centerline – the mid-line separating the service courts.

- Clear – a high shot that goes over the opponent's head and lands close to the baseline.

- Combination alignment – partners playing both up-and-back and side-by-side during doubles games and/or volleys.

- Crosscourt – a diagonal shot hit into the opposite court.

- Defense – the team or player hitting the shuttle upwards.

- Double hit – an illegal shot where the player contacts the shuttle twice with the racket in one swing.

- Doubles service court – the short, wide area to which the server must serve in doubles play.

- Down-the-line shot – a straight-ahead shot (usually down the sideline).

- Drive – a hard, driven shot traveling parallel to the floor (clears the net but does not have enough height for opponent to smash).

- Drop – a shot just clearing the net and then falling close to it.

- Face – the racket's string area.

- Fault – an infraction of the rules resulting in loss of serve or a point awarded to the server.

- First serve – a term used in doubles play to indicate that the server is the "first server" during an inning.

- Foot fault – Illegal movement/position of the feet by either the server or receiver.

- Forecourt – the front area of the court (between the net and the short service line).

- Forehand – a stroke made on the racket side of the body.

- Game point – the point, if won, that allows the server to win the game.

- Hand in – a term indicating that the server retains the serve.

- Hand out – the term used in doubles to denote that one player has lost the service.

- Home base – a center court position where a player can best play any shot hit by an opponent.

- Inning – the period a player or team holds service.

- Let – stopping the point because of some type of outside interference. The point is replayed.

- Lifting the shuttle – stroking the shuttle underhanded and hitting it upward.

- Long serve – a high, deep serve landing near the long service line in doubles or the back boundary line in singles.

- Love – the term used to indicate a zero score.

- Match – a series of games. Winning two out of three games wins the match.

- Match point – the point, if won by the server, making him the winner of the match.

- Midcourt – the middle-third of the court (between short service line and long service line for doubles).

- Net shot – a shot taken near the net.

- Non-racket side – the opposite side of the hand holding the racket.

- Offense – the team or player that is stroking the shuttle downward.

- Overhead – a motion used to strike the shuttle when it is above the head.

- Racket foot or leg – the foot or leg on the same side as the hand holding the racket.

- Ready position – the position a player assumes to be able to move in any direction.

- Receiver – the player to whom the shuttle is served.

- Second serve – in doubles, the term indicates that one partner has lost the serve, and the other partner is now serving.

- Server – the player putting the shuttle into play.

- Setting – choosing the amount of additional points to play when certain tie scores are reached.

- Short-serve – a serve barely clearing the net and landing just beyond the short service line.

- Shuttlecock/Shuttle – the feathered, plastic or nylon object that is volleyed back and forth over the net.

- Side Alley – see alley.

- Smash – an overhead stroke hit downward with great velocity and angle.

- "T" – the intersection of the centerline and the short service line.

- Underhand – an upward stroke to hit the shuttle when it has fallen below shoulder level.

- Unsight – illegal position taken by the server's partner so the receiver cannot see the shuttle being hit.

- Up-and-back – an offensive alignment used in doubles. The "up" player is responsible for the forecourt and the "back" player is responsible for both.

BASKETBALL TERMINOLOGY:

- Backcourt players (Guards) – players who set up a team's offensive pattern and bring the ball up the court.

- Backdoor – an offensive maneuver in which a player cuts towards the baseline to the basket, behind the defenders, and receives a ball for a field goal attempt.

- Baseline – the end line of the court.

- Blocking/Boxing out – a term used when a player is positioned under the backboard to prevent an opposing player from achieving a good rebounding position.

- Charging – personal contact by a player with the ball against the body of a defensive opponent.

- Corner players (Forwards) – tall players that make up the sides of the offensive set-up who are responsible for the rebounding and shooting phases of the team's offense.

- Cut – a quick, offensive move by a player attempting to get free for a pass.

- Denial defense – aggressive individual defense to keep an offensive player from receiving a pass.

- Double foul – two opponents committing personal fouls against each other simultaneously.

- Dribble – ball movement by a player in control who throws or taps the ball in the air or onto the floor and then touches it. The dribble ends when the dribbler touches the ball with both hands concurrently, loses control, or permits it to come to rest while in contact with it.

- Drive – an aggressive move by a player with the ball towards the basket.

- Fake (Feint) – using a deceptive move with the ball pulling the defensive player out of position.

- Fast break – quickly moving the ball down court to score before the defense has a chance to set up.

- Field goal – a basket scored from the field.

- Freelance – no structure or set plays in the offense.

- Free throw – the right given to a player to score one or two points by unhindered shots for a basket from within the free throw circle and behind the free throw line.

- Give-and-go – a maneuver when the offensive player passes to a teammate and then immediately cuts in toward the basket for a return pass.

- Held ball – occurs when two opponents have one or both hands firmly on the ball and neither can gain possession without undue roughness.

- Inside player (Center, Post, Pivot) – this player is usually the tallest player in the team who is situated near the basket, around the three-second lane area, and is responsible for rebounding and close-range shooting.

- Jump ball – a method of putting the ball into play by tossing it up between two opponents in the center circle to start the game or any overtime periods.

- Outlet pass – a term used that designates a direct pass from a rebounder to a teammate (the main objective is starting a fast break).

- Overtime period – an additional period of playing time when the score is tied at the end of the regulation game.

- Personal foul – a player foul that involves contact with an opponent while the ball is alive or after the ball is in possession of a player for a throw-in.

- Pick – a special type of screen where a player stands so that the defensive player slides to make contact to free an offensive teammate for a shot or drive.

- Pivot – occurs when a player who is holding the ball steps once or more than once in any direction with the same foot while the other foot, called the pivot foot, remains at its point of contact with the floor. Also, another term for the inside player.

- Posting up – a player cutting to the three-second lane area, pausing, and anticipating a pass.

- Rebound – when the ball bounces off the backboard or basket.

- Restraining circles – three circles with a six-foot radius. One is located in the center of the court, and the others are located at each of the free-throw lines.

- Running time – not stopping the clock for fouls or violations.

- Screen – an offensive maneuver positioning a player between the defender and a teammate to free the teammate for an uncontested shot.

- Switching – defensive guards reversing their guarding assignments.

- Technical foul – a non-contact foul by a player, team, or coach for unsportsmanlike behavior or failing to abide by rules regarding submission of lineups, uniform numbering, and substitution procedures.

- Telegraphing a pass – a look or signal to indicate where the ball is going to be passed.

- Throw-in – a method of putting the ball in play from out-of-bounds.

- Traveling – illegal movement, in any direction, of a player in possession of the ball within bounds. Moving with the ball without dribbling.

- Violation – an infraction of the rules resulting in a throw-in from out-of-bounds.

BOWLING TERMINOLOGY:

- Anchor – the teammate who shoots last.

- Baby split – the 1-7 or 3-10 pin railroads.

- Backup – a reverse hook rotating to the right for a right-handed bowler.

- Bed posts – the 7-10 railroad.

- Blow – an error or missing a spare that is not split.

- Box – a frame.

- Brooklyn – a crossover ball striking the 1-2 pocket.

- Bucket – the 2-4-5-8 or 3-5-6-9 leaves.

- Cherry – chopping off the front pin on a spare.

- Double – two consecutive strikes.

- Double pinochle – the 7-6 and 4-10 split.

- Crossover – same as a Brooklyn.

- Dutch 200 (Dutchman) – a score of 200 made by alternating strikes and spares for the entire game.

- Error – same as a "blow."

- Foul – touching or going beyond the foul line in delivering the ball.

- Frame – the box where scores are entered.

- Gutter ball – a ball that falls into either gutter.

- Handicap – awarding an individual or team a bonus score or score adjustment that is based on averages.

- Head pin – the number one pin.

- Hook – a ball that breaks to the left for a right-handed bowler and breaks to the right for a left-handed bowler.

- Jersey side – same as a Brooklyn.

- Kegler – synonym for a bowler.

- Lane – a bowling alley.

- Leave – pin or pins left standing after a throw.

- Light hit – hitting the head pin lightly to the right or left side.

- Line – a complete game as recorded on the score sheet.

- Mark – getting a strike or spare.

- Open frame – a frame in which no mark is made, leaving at least one pin standing after rolling both balls in a frame.

- Pocket – space between the head pin and pins on either side.

- Railroad – synonym for a split.

- Sleeper – a pin hidden from view.

- Spare – knocking all pins down with two balls.

- Split – a leave, after throwing the first ball, in which the number one pin plus a second pin are down, and when seven pins remain standing.

- Spot – a bowler's point of aim on the alley.

- Striking out – obtaining three strikes in the last frame.

- Tap – a pin that remains standing after an apparently perfect hit.

- Turkey – three consecutive strikes.

RACQUETBALL/HANDBALL TERMINOLOGY:

- Ace – a serve that completely eludes the receiver.

- Back-wall shot – a shot made from a rebound off the back wall.

- Box – see service box.

- Ceiling shot – a shot that first strikes the ceiling, then the front wall.

- Crotch – the junction of any two playing surfaces, as between the floor and any wall.

- Crotch shot – a ball that simultaneously strikes the front wall and floor (not good).

- Cut throat – a three-man game in which the server plays against the other two players. Each player keeps an individual score.

- Drive shot – a power shot against the front wall rebounding in a fast, low, and straight line.

- Fault – an illegally served ball.

- Handout – retiring the server who fails to serve legally or when the serving team fails to return a ball that is in play.

- Hinder – interference or obstruction of the flight of the ball during play.

- Kill – a ball rebounded off the front wall so close to the floor that it is impossible to return.

- Passing shot – a shot placed out of an opponent's reach on either side.

- Rally – continuous play of the ball by opponents.

- Receiving line – the broken line parallel to the short line on a racquetball court.

- Run-around shot – a ball striking one sidewall, the rear wall, and the other sidewall.

- Safety zone – a five-foot area bounded by the back edge of the short line and receiving line that is only observed during the serve in racquetball.

- Screen – a hinder due to obstruction of the opponent's vision.

- Server – person in the "hand-in" position and eligible to serve.

- Service box – the service zone bounded by the sidewall and a parallel line 18 inches away; denotes where server's partner must stand in doubles during the serve.

- Service court – the area where the ball must land when it is returned from the front wall on the serve.

- Service line – the line that is parallel to and five feet in front of the short line.

- Service zone – the area where the ball must be served.

- Short line – the line on the floor parallel to front wall and equidistant from front and back wall. The serve must go over this line when returning from the front wall.

- Shoot – attempt kill shots.

- Side out – loss of serve.

- Thong – the strap on the bottom handle of the racquetball racquet that is worn around the player's wrist.

- Volley – returning the ball to the front wall before it bounces on the floor.

- Z-ball – defensive shot that strikes the front wall, a sidewall, and then the opposite sidewall.

SOCCER TERMINOLOGY:

- Center – passing from the outside of the field near the sideline into the center.

- Charge – illegal or legal body contact between opponents.

- Chip – lofting the ball into the air using the instep kick technique; contacting the ball very low causing it to loft quickly with backspin.

- Clear – attempting to move the ball out of danger by playing the ball a great distance.

- Corner kick – a direct free kick from the corner arc awarded to the attacking player when the defending team last played the ball over their own end line.

- Cross – a pass from the outside of the field near the end line to a position in front of the goal.

- Dead ball situation – the organized restarting of the game after stopping play.

- Direct free kick – a free kick whereby the kicker may score immediately from the initial contact.

- Dribble – the technique of a player self-propelling the ball with the foot in order to maintain control of the ball while moving from one spot to another.

- Drop ball – the method used to restart the game after temporary suspension of play when the ball is still in play.

- Goal area – the rectangular area in front of the goal where the ball is placed for a goal kick.

- Half volley – contacting the ball just as it hits the ground after being airborne.

- Head – playing the ball with the head.

- Indirect free kick – a free kick from which a player, other than the kicker, must contact the ball before a goal can be scored.

- Kickoff – the free kick starting play at the beginning of the game, after each period, or after a score.

- Obstruction – illegally using the body to shield an opponent from reaching the ball.

- One-touch – immediately passing or shooting a received ball without stopping it.

- Penalty area – the large rectangular area in front of the goal where the goalkeeper is allowed to use his hands to play the ball.

- Penalty kick – a direct free kick awarded in the penalty area against the defending team for a Direct Free Kick foul.

- Settle – taking a ball out of the air and settling it on the ground so that it is rolling and no longer bouncing.

- Square pass – a pass directed towards the side of a player.

- Tackle – a technique to take the ball away from the opponents.

- Through pass – a pass penetrating between and past the defenders.

- Throw-in – the technique to restart the game when the ball goes out of play over the sideline.

- Touchline – the side line of the field.

- Trap – the technique used for receiving the ball and bringing it under control.

- Two-touch- receiving – trapping and immediately re-passing the ball.

TENNIS TERMINOLOGY:

- Ace – serving a ball untouched by the opponent's racket.

- Advantage (Ad) – a scoring term. The next point won after the score is "deuce."

- Alley – the 4.5-foot strip on either side of the singles court that is used to enlarge the court for doubles.

- Approach shot – a shot hit inside the baseline while approaching the net.

- Backcourt – the area between the service line and the baseline.

- Backhand – strokes hit on the left side of a right-handed player.

- Backspin – spin placed on a ball that causes the ball to bounce back towards the hitter.

- Back swing – the beginning of all ground strokes and service motion requiring a back swing to gather energy for the forward swing.

- Baseline – the end line of a tennis court.

- Break – winning a game when the opponent serves.

- Center mark – a short mark bisecting the baseline.

- Center service line – the line perpendicular to the net dividing the two service courts in halves.

- Center strap – the strap at the center of the net anchored to the court to facilitate a constant 3-foot height for the net at its center.

- Center stripe – same as the center service line.

- Chip – a short chopping motion of the racket against the back and bottom side of the ball imparting backspin.

- Chop – placing backspin on the ball with a short, high-to-low forward swing.

- Cross-court – a shot hit diagonally from one corner of the court over the net into the opposite corner of the court.

- Cut off the angle – moving forward quickly against an opponent's cross-court shot, allowing the player to hit the ball near the center of the court rather than near the sidelines.

- Deep (depth) – a shot bouncing near the baseline on ground strokes and near the service line on serves.

- Default – a player who forfeits his/her position in a tournament by not playing a scheduled match.

- Deuce – a term used when the game score is 40-40.

- Dink – a ball hit very softly and relatively high to ensure its safe landing.

- Double fault – two consecutive out-of-bounds serves on the same point resulting in loss of the point.

- Doubles lines – the outside sidelines on a court used only for doubles.

- Down-the-line – a shot hit near a sideline traveling close to, and parallel to, the same line from which the shot was initially hit.

- Drive – an offensive shot hit with extra force.

- Drop shot – a ground stroke hit so that it drops just over the net with little or no forward bounce.

- Drop volley – a volley hit in such a manner that it drops just over the net with little or no forward bounce.

- Error – a mistake made by a player during competition.

- Flat shot – a ball hit so there is no rotation or spin when traveling through the air.

- Foot fault – illegal foot movement before service, penalized by losing that particular serve. Common foot faults are: stepping on or ahead of the baseline before the ball has been contacted and running along the baseline before serving.

- Forecourt – the area between the net and the service line.

- Forehand – the stroke hit on the right side of a right-handed player.

- Frame – the rim of the racket head plus the handle of the racket.

- Game – scoring term when a player wins 4 points before an opponent while holding a minimum 2-point lead.

- Grip – the portion of the racket that is grasped in the player's hand.

- Groundstroke – any ball hit after it has bounced.

- Half volley – a ball hit inches away from the court's surface after the ball has bounced.

- Hold serve – winning your own serve. If you lose your own serve, your serve has been "broken."

- Let (ball) – a point replayed because of some kind of interference.

- Let serve – a serve that touches the net tape, falls into the proper square, and is played over.

- Linesman – a match official who calls balls "in" or "out."

- Lob – a ball hit with sufficient height to pass over the out-stretched arm of a net player.

- Lob volley – a shot hit high into the air from a volleying position.

- Love – scoring term that means zero points or games.

- Match – a contest between two or four opponents.

- Match point – the point prior to the final point of a match.

- Midcourt – the area in front of the baseline or behind the service line of the playing court.

- Net ball – a ball that hits the net, falling on the same side as the hitter.

- No man's land – a general area within the baseline and proper net position area. When caught in that area, the player must volley or hit ground strokes near his/her feet.

- Offensive lob – a ball hit just above the racket reach of an opposing net player.

- Open face racket – a racket whose face is moving under the ball. A wide-open racket face is parallel to the court surface.

- Overhead – a shot hit from a position higher than the player's head.

- Over-hitting – hitting shots with too much force; over-hitting usually results in errors.

- Pace – the speed of the ball.

- Passing shot – a shot passing beyond the reach of the net player landing inbounds.

- Poach – to cross over into your partner's territory in doubles in an attempt to intercept the ball.

- Racket face – the racket's hitting surface.

- Racket head – the top portion of the racket frame that includes the strings.

- Rally – opponents hitting balls back and forth across the net.

- Receiver – the player about to return the opponent's serve.

- Server – the player initiating play.

- Service line – the line at the end of the service courts parallel to the net.

- Set – a scoring term meaning the first player to win six games with a minimum two-game lead.

- Set point – the point, if won, which will give the player the set.

- Sidespin – a ball hit rotating on a horizontal plane.

- Signals in doubles – signaling your partner that you are going to poach at the net.

- Singles line – the sideline closest to the center mark that runs the entire length of the court.

- Slice – motion of the racket head going around the side of the ball, producing a horizontal spin on the ball.

- Tape – the band of cloth or plastic running across the top of the net.

- Telegraphing the play – indicating the direction of one's intended target before hitting the ball.

- Topspin – forward rotation of the ball.

- Touch – the ability to make delicate, soft shots from several positions on the court.

- Twist – a special rotation applied to the ball during the serve causing the ball to jump to the left (of right-handed server).

- Umpire – the official that calls lines.

- Under spin – a counterclockwise spin placed on the ball (i.e. backspin).

- Volley – hitting the ball in the air before it bounces on the court.

VOLLEYBALL TERMINOLOGY:

- Attack – returning the ball across the net in an attempt to put the opponents at a disadvantage.

- Ball handling – executing any passing fundamental.

- Block – intercepting the ball just before or as it crosses the net.

- Bump – see forearm pass.

- Court coverage – a defensive player's court assignment.

- Dig – an emergency pass usually used to defend a hard-driven attack.

- Dink – a soft shot off the fingertips to lob the ball over a block.

- Double foul – infraction of rules by both teams during the same play.

- Drive – an attacking shot contacted in the center that attempts to hit the ball off the blocker's hands.

- Fault – any infraction of the rules.

- Forearm pass – a pass made off the forearms that is used to play served balls, hard-driven spikes, or any low ball.

- Free ball – a ball returned by the opponent that is easily handled.

- Frontcourt – the playing area where it is legal to block or attack.

- Held ball – a ball that is simultaneously contacted above the net by opponents and momentarily held upon contact.

- Kill – an attack that cannot be returned.

- Lob – a soft attack contacted on the back bottom-quarter of the ball causing an upward trajectory.

- Overhand pass – a pass made by contacting the ball above the head with the fingers.

- Overlap – an illegal foot position when the ball is dead, with an adjacent player putting another out of position.

- Play over – replaying the rally because of a held ball or the official prematurely suspending play. The server re-serves with no point awarded.

- **Point** – a point is scored when the receiving team fails to legally return the ball to the opponents' court.

- **Rotation** – clockwise rotation of the players upon gaining the ball from the opponents.

- **Serve** – putting the ball in play over the net by striking it with the hand.

- **Set** – placing the ball near the net to facilitate attacking.

- **Setter** – the player assigned to set the ball.

- **Side out** – side is out when the serving team fails to win a point or plays the ball illegally.

- **Spike** – a ball hit with top spin and with a strong downward force into the opponents' court.

- **Spiker** – the player assigned to attack the ball.

- **Spike-roll** – an attack that first takes an upward trajectory using the spiking action (with or without jumping).

- **Topspin (Overspin)** – applying forward spin to the ball during the serve, spike, or spike roll.

APPROPRIATE OFFICIATING TECHNIQUES IN SPORT SITUATIONS

NOTE: Since rules change yearly, acquiring new rulebooks every year is necessary for officiating properly.

BASKETBALL SITUATION: Actions of the spectators interfere with the progression of the game.

- **Ruling:** An official may call a foul on the team whose supporters interfering with the game.

BASKETBALL SITUATION: The official in the frontcourt runs into a pass thrown from the backcourt by A1 and the ball goes out-of-bounds.

- **Ruling:** Throw-in is awarded to B.

BASKETBALL SITUATION: A1 catches the ball in mid-air and lands with the right foot first and then the left foot. A1 pivots on the left foot.

- **Ruling:** A violation has occurred because A1 can only pivot on the foot that first lands on the floor, which was the right foot.

SOCCER SITUATION: The ball is alive when a substitute enters the playing field.

- **Ruling:** A non-player foul has occurred. Referee can either penalize at the location of the next dead ball or at the place of entry (usually where the team that is offended is at an advantage).

SOCCER SITUATION: A1 goalie, in own penalty area, is charged by B1.

- **Ruling:** Team A is awarded a direct free kick at the spot of foul. A flagrant charge awards team A penalty-kick at the other end of the field, and B1 is disqualified.

SOCCER SITUATION: The goalie is out of position when a back on team B heads the ball out and it falls into the net. A2 gets the ball, passes it to A1, and has only the goalie to beat.

- **Ruling:** A1 is not offside because the B back left the field during legal play.

VOLLEYBALL SITUATION: Team A's second volley hits an obstruction directly over the net, returns to A's playing area, and is again played by team A.

- **Ruling:** Fair play and the next play is team A's third play.

VOLLEYBALL SITUATION: The serving team has three front line players standing close together in front of the server at the spiking line.

- **Ruling:** Illegal alignment and is called for intentional screening.

VOLLEYBALL SITUATION: RB and CB on the receiving team are overlapping when the ball is contacted for the serve, and the serve lands out-of-bounds.

- **Ruling:** Serving team is awarded a point because of receiving team's illegal alignment.

VOLLEYBALL SITUATION: LB on team B saves a spiked ball and it deflects off his/her shoulder.

- **Ruling:** A legal hit.

TEACHER CERTIFICATION STUDY GUIDE

ACTIONS THAT PROMOTE SAFETY

1. Having an instructor who is properly trained and qualified.

2. Organizing the class by size, activity, and conditions of the class.

3. Inspecting buildings and other facilities regularly and immediately giving notice of any hazards.

4. Avoiding overcrowding.

5. Using adequate lighting.

6. Ensuring that students dress in appropriate clothing and shoes.

7. Presenting organized activities.

8. Inspecting all equipment regularly.

9. Adhering to building codes and fire regulations.

10. Using protective equipment.

11. Using spotters.

12. Eliminating hazards.

13. Teaching students correct ways of performing skills and activities.

14. Teaching students how to use the equipment properly and safely.

AQUATIC SKILLS

Water safety issues include student's familiarity with appropriate medical responses to life-threatening situations. Students should recognize signs that someone needs medical attention (e.g. not moving, not breathing, etc.) and have knowledge of the proper response (e.g. who to contact and where to find them). With older children, the instructor can introduce rudimentary first aid. The instructor must also ensure that students are aware and observant of safety rules (e.g. no running near the water, no chewing gum while swimming, no swimming without a lifeguard, no roughhousing near or in the water, etc.).

Swimming strokes include Butterfly, Breast Stroke, Crawl, Sidestroke, Trudgen, Freestyle, Backstroke, and Dog Paddle. When teaching children how to dive, emphasis should be placed on form (arm and body alignment) and safety procedures (e.g. no diving in the shallow end, no pushing students into the water).

OUTDOOR EDUCATION

Techniques and skills include:

- **Walking and Hiking** – Instructors can take students on walking/hiking trips through nature reserves and national parks. Such trips can incorporate team-building activities and nature education.

- **Rope Challenge Courses** – Good activity for team-building purposes. Challenges include personal physical challenges (climbing various structures), or group activities (e.g. requiring students to work together to coordinate the crossing of a course). Safety requirements include helmets, harnesses, spotters, trained supervisors, and strict adherence to all safety procedures and educator instructions.

- **Sail Training** – Students taught to sail should display competence in the maintenance and piloting of a boat, including cooperative activities necessary to a successful sailing endeavor (e.g. working together to get the boat into and out of the water, paddling in rhythm, turning the boat, etc.). Prior to the start of sail training, students should understand all safety procedures and acceptable forms of behavior on a boat (e.g. only standing when necessary, no pushing, following instructions, wearing a life jacket, etc.). Students must also demonstrate swimming competence (i.e. ability to tread water, swim a distance continuously, and put on a life jacket while in the water).

Related safety education should emphasize the importance of planning and research. Students should consider in advance what the potential dangers of an activity might be and to prepare plans accordingly (students and instructors should also examine weather forecasts). Of course, educator supervision is required. First-aid equipment and well trained educators must be present for outdoor education activities. Students should use proper safety gear when appropriate (e.g. helmets, harnesses, etc.). Parental consent is generally required for outdoor education activities.

COMBATIVE ACTIVITIES

Basic knowledge of wrestling includes knowledge of basic techniques (familiarity with pins, reversals, and positioning transitions), drills for practicing technique (e.g. students can drill shooting and sprawling, drill reversals from pinned positions, etc.), and terminology (naming the techniques, e.g. shoot, sprawl, half-nelson, full-nelson, etc.).

Basic knowledge of self-defense includes familiarity with basic striking techniques (punches and kicks), blocks and evasions, knowledge of major vital points on the body (eyes, nose, ears, jaw, throat, solar plexus, groin, knees, instep), knowledge of basic escape techniques (from chokes, grabs and bear-hugs) and some situational training (to prevent 'freezing' in a real-life encounter). Martial arts (e.g. judo, karate) are common forms of self-defense that physical education instructors can teach to students.

In-class focus should be placed on strategies for conflict recognition (based on developing an understanding of threat factors, like individuals in a hostile frame of mind), avoidance (physically avoiding potentially dangerous situations), and diffusion (overview of the psychology of confrontations, evaluation of the motivations behind a hostile encounter, understanding of the way body language and eye contact can impact the situation).

Related safety issues include stressing the potential harm that can result from the techniques being practiced (stressing specific damage potential to musculoskeletal systems), emphasizing students' responsibility for the well-being of their training partners, maintaining discipline throughout the class (ensuring students remain focused on their training activities and alert to the educator's instructions), and ensuring that students are aware and observant of the limits to force that they may apply (no-striking zones, like above the neck and below the belt; limits on striking force, like semi-contact or no-contact sparring; familiarity with the concept of a tap-out indicating submission). Students should perform warm-up, cool-down, and stretching as with any physical training program.

LIFETIME ACTIVITIES AND RECREATIONAL PURSUITS

Many lifetime activities and recreational pursuits involve physical activity, games, and sports. Some sports, such as tennis and golf, are lifetime activities. Healthy individuals can participate in such lifetime sports well into their 80's and even 90's. Other recreational pursuits, such as hiking, boating, walking, jogging, and bicycling, are important parts of many people's lives. Such pursuits provide recreation, enjoyment, social interaction, and physical fitness to participants. The physical education instructor should introduce students to activities and pursuits that promote lifetime participation and activity.

PROPER USE OF EQUIPMENT, FACILITIES, SPACE, AND COMMUNITY RESOURCES

In addition to providing a safe, education-friendly environment that maximizes the use of class time, physical education instructors must effectively use equipment, facilities, space, and community resources.

Instructors must have a thorough understanding of athletic equipment to demonstrate proper usage to students and ensure student safety during activities. Instructors should expose students to a variety of activities and related equipment. Instructors must also consider the feasibility of certain activities as determined by the availability and costliness of equipment.

Instructors must consider available facilities and space when planning physical education curriculum. Facilities and space may limit the type of activities students can engage in. For example, sports like golf require large open spaces and specific equipment which schools may not have access to.

Finally, physical education instructors should investigate and research community resources. Community organizations and athletic clubs often will provide equipment, facilities, and volunteer instructors to schools at reduced or no cost.

CARE AND MAINTENANCE PROCEDURES FOR FACILITIES AND EQUIPMENT

Facilities and equipment are basic components of every physical education program. However, such facilities and equipment regular maintenance to sustain longevity and safety features.

Schools, clubs, gyms, and other centers have facilities, such as sport and exercise equipment, that require regular care to prevent injuries to users. Instructors must check fields and equipment carefully and on a consistent basis. Instructors must repair outdated, worn-out, or defective physical education machines to ensure student safety. In order to avoid serious problems, instructors must remove faulty equipment.

Outdoor facilities should also have a system by which authorities and other officials in charge can inform participants to take shelter in case of dangerous and threatening weather conditions. All authorities, such as schools, public authorities, and governments, should take responsibility in promoting proper installation of appropriate equipment and the overall safety of physical education facilities.

COMPETENCY 3.0   FITNESS AND EXERCISE SCIENCE

SKILL 3.1   Components: cardiorespiratory and muscular endurance, body composition, flexibility

HEALTH-RELATED COMPONENTS OF PHYSICAL FITNESS

There are five health related components of physical fitness: **cardio-respiratory or cardiovascular endurance, muscle strength, muscle endurance, flexibility, and body composition.**

Cardiovascular endurance – the ability of the body to sustain aerobic activities (activities requiring oxygen utilization) for extended periods.

Muscle strength – the ability of muscle groups to contract and support a given amount of weight.

Muscle endurance – the ability of muscle groups to contract continually over a period of time and support a given amount of weight.

Flexibility – the ability of muscle groups to stretch and bend.

Body composition – an essential measure of health and fitness. The most important aspects of body composition are body fat percentage and ratio of body fat to muscle.

Wellness has two major components: understanding the basic human body functions and how to care for and maintain personal fitness. Developing an awareness and knowledge on how certain everyday factors, stress and personal decisions can affect one's health. Teaching fitness needs to go along with skill and activity instruction. Life-long fitness and the benefits of a healthy lifestyle need to be part of every P.E. teacher's curriculum. Cross-discipline teaching and teaching thematically with other subject matter in classrooms would be the ideal method to teach health to adolescents.

Incorporating wellness into the P.E. teacher's lesson plan doesn't need to take that much time or effort. For example, have students understand the idea that if you put more calories in your body than what you burn, you will gain weight. Teaching nutrition and the caloric content of foods in P.E. can be as simple as learning the amount of calories burned when participating in different sports for a set amount of time. When teaching a more sophisticated lesson on nutrition which helps students understand the relationship between caloric intake and caloric expenditure, students could keep a food diary, tabulating the caloric content of their own diets while comparing it to an exercise diary that keeps track of the calories they've burned.

Another example of incorporating wellness into the P.E. curriculum would be during endurance running activities. Having students run a set distance and giving them a finish time, rewards the faster students and defeats the slower students. In addition to a final time, students must be taught a more beneficial way of measuring one's cardiovascular fitness by understanding pulse rate.

Teach students how to take their own pulse, how pulse rates vary at different stages of exercise (i.e. resting pulse, target pulse, recovery pulse, etc.), how pulse rates can differ between boys and girls, and encourage them to keep track of their own figures. As students gather their data, teacher-led discussions amongst classmates about similarities, differences and patterns that are developing would teach students how to monitor effectively and easily their own vital signs.

VALID PHYSICAL FITNESS TEST ITEMS TO MEASURE HEALTH RELATED FITNESS COMPONENTS

The following is a list of tests that instructors can use to assess the physical fitness of students.

Cardio-respiratory fitness tests – maximal stress test, sub maximal stress test, Bruce Protocol, Balke Protocol, Astrand and Rhyming Test, PWC Test, Bench Step Test, Rockport Walking Fitness Test, and Cooper 1.5 Mile Run/Walk Fitness Test.

Muscle strength tests – dynamometers (hand, back, and leg), cable tensiometer, the 1-RM Test (repetition maximum: bench press, standing press, arm curl, and leg press), bench-squat, sit-ups (one sit up holding a weight plate behind the neck), and lateral pull-down.

Muscle endurance tests – squat-thrust, pull-ups, sit-ups, lateral pull-down, bench-press, arm curl, push-ups, and dips.

Flexibility tests – sit and reach, Kraus-Webber Floor Touch Test, trunk extension, forward bend of trunk, Leighton Flexometer, shoulder rotation/flexion, and goniometer.

Body Composition determination – Hydrostatic weighing, skin fold measurements, limb/girth circumference, and body mass index.

SKILL 3.2   Conditioning practices and principles: frequency, intensity, time/duration, the role of exercise

BASIC TRAINING PRINCIPLES

The **Overload Principle** is exercising at an above normal level to improve physical or physiological capacity (a higher than normal workload).

The **Specificity Principle** is overloading a particular fitness component. In order to improve a component of fitness, you must isolate and specifically work on a single component. Metabolic and physiological adaptations depend on the type of overload; hence, specific exercise produces specific adaptations, creating specific training effects.

The **Progression Principle** states that once the body adapts to the original load/stress, no further improvement of a component of fitness will occur without an additional load.

There is also a **Reversibility-of-Training Principle** in which all gains in fitness are lost with the discontinuance of a training program.

MODIFICATIONS OF OVERLOAD

We can modify overload by varying **frequency, intensity, and time**. Frequency is the number of times we implement a training program in a given period (e.g. three days per week). Intensity is the amount of effort put forth or the amount of stress placed on the body. Time is the duration of each training session.

TARGET HEART RATE ZONE

The target heart rate (THR) zone is a common measure of aerobic exercise intensity. Participants find their THR and attempt to raise their heart rate to the desired level for a certain period of time. There are three ways to calculate the target heart rate.

1. METs (maximum oxygen uptake), which is 60% to 90% of functional capacity.

2. Karvonean Formula = [Maximum heart rate (MHR) − Resting heart rate (RHR)] x intensity + RHR.   MHR= 220 - Age
Intensity = Target Heart Range (which is 60% - 80% of MHR - RHR + RHR).
THR = (MHR - RHR) x .60 + RHR to (MHR - RHR) x .80 + RHR

3. Cooper's Formula to determine target heart range is:
THR = (220 - AGE) x .60 to (220 - AGE) x .80.

PRINCIPLES OF OVERLOAD, PROGRESSION, AND SPECIFICITY APPLIED TO IMPROVEMENT OF HEALTH-RELATED COMPONENTS OF FITNESS

1. Cardio-respiratory Fitness:

Overloading for cardio-respiratory fitness:

- **Frequency** = minimum of 3 days/week
- **Intensity** = exercising in target heart-rate zone
- **Time** = minimum of 20 minutes

Progression for cardiovascular fitness:

- begin at a frequency of 3 days/week and work up to no more than 6 days/week
- begin at an intensity near THR threshold and work up to 80% of THR
- begin at 20 minutes and work up to 60 minutes

Specificity for cardiovascular fitness:

- To develop cardiovascular fitness, you must perform aerobic (with oxygen) activities for at least fifteen minutes without developing an oxygen debt. Aerobic activities include, but are not limited to brisk walking, jogging, bicycling, and swimming.

2. Muscle Strength:

Overloading for muscle strength:

- **Frequency** = every other day
- **Intensity** = 60% to 90% of assessed muscle strength
- **Time** = 3 sets of 3 - 8 reps (high resistance with a low number of repetitions)

Progression for muscle strength:

- begin 3 days/week and work up to every other day
- begin near 60% of determined muscle strength and work up to no more than 90% of muscle strength
- begin with 1 set with 3 reps and work up to 3 sets with 8 reps

Specificity for muscle strength:

- to increase muscle strength for a specific part(s) of the body, you must target that/those part(s) of the body

3. Muscle endurance:

Overloading for muscle endurance:

- **Frequency** = every other day
- **Intensity** = 30% to 60% of assessed muscle strength
- **Time** = 3 sets of 12 - 20 reps (low resistance with a high number of repetitions)

Progression for muscle endurance:

- begin 3 days/week and work up to every other day
- begin at 20% to 30% of muscle strength and work up to no more than 60% of muscle strength
- begin with 1 set with 12 reps and work up to 3 sets with 20 reps

Specificity for muscle endurance:

- same as muscle strength

4. Flexibility:

Overloading for flexibility:

- **Frequency**: 3 to 7 days/week
- **Intensity**: stretch muscle beyond its normal length
- **Time**: 3 sets of 3 reps holding stretch for 15 to 60 seconds

Progression for flexibility:

- begin 3 days/week and work up to every day
- begin stretching with slow movement as far as possible without pain, holding at the end of the range of motion (ROM) and work up to stretching no more than 10% beyond the normal ROM

- begin with 1 set with 1 rep, holding stretches for 15 seconds, and work up to 3 sets with 3 reps, holding stretches for 60 seconds

Specificity for flexibility:

- ROM is joint specific

5. Body composition:

Overloading to improve body composition:

- **Frequency**: daily aerobic exercise
- **Intensity**: low
- **Time**: approximately one hour

Progression to improve body composition:

- begin daily
- begin a low aerobic intensity and work up to a longer duration (see cardio-respiratory progression)
- begin low-intensity aerobic exercise for 30 minutes and work up to 60 minutes

Specificity to improve body composition:

- increase aerobic exercise and decrease caloric intake

PRINCIPLES AND ACTIVITIES FOR DEVELOPING AEROBIC ENDURANCE

The term aerobic refers to conditioning or exercise that requires the use of oxygen to derive energy. Aerobic conditioning is essential for fat loss, energy production, and effective functioning of the cardiovascular system. Aerobic exercise is difficult to perform for many people and participants must follow certain principles and activities in order to develop aerobic endurance.

Tips that aid in developing and building aerobic endurance include working out for extended periods at the target heart rate, slowly increasing aerobic exercises, exercising for three or four times per week, and taking adequate rest to help the body recover.

ROLE OF EXERCISE IN HEALTH MAINTENANCE

The health risk factors improved by physical activity include: cholesterol levels, blood pressure, stress related disorders, heart diseases, weight and obesity disorders, early death, certain types of cancer, musculoskeletal problems, mental health, and susceptibility to infectious diseases. The following is a list of physical activities that may reduce some of these health risks.

1. **Aerobic Dance:**
Health-related components of fitness = *cardio-respiratory, body composition.*
Skill-related components of fitness = *agility, coordination.*

2. **Bicycling:**
Health-related components of fitness = *cardio-respiratory, muscle strength, muscle endurance, body composition.*
Skill-related components of fitness = *balance.*

3. **Calisthenics:**
Health-related components of fitness = *cardio-respiratory, muscle strength, muscle endurance, flexibility, body composition.*
Skill-related components of fitness = *agility.*

4. **Circuit Training:**
Health-related components of fitness = *cardio-respiratory, muscle strength, muscle endurance, body composition.*
Skill-related components of fitness = *power.*

5. **Cross Country Skiing:**
Health-related component of fitness = *cardio-respiratory, muscle strength, muscle endurance, body composition.*
Skill-related components of fitness = *agility, coordination, power.*

6. **Jogging/Running:**
Health-related components of fitness = *cardio-respiratory, body composition.*

7. **Rope Jumping:**
Health-related components of fitness = *cardio-respiratory, body composition.*
Skill-related components of fitness = *agility, coordination, reaction time, speed.*

8. **Rowing:**
Health-related components of fitness = *cardio-respiratory, muscle strength, muscle endurance, body composition.*
Skill-related components of fitness = *agility, coordination, power.*

9. **Skating:**
Health-related components of fitness = *cardio-respiratory, body composition.*
Skill-related components of fitness = *agility, balance, coordination, speed.*

10. **Swimming/Water Exercises**:
Health-related components of fitness = *cardio-respiratory, muscle strength, muscle endurance, flexibility, body composition.*
Skill related components of fitness = *agility, coordination.*

11. **Walking (brisk)**:
Health-related components of fitness = *cardio-respiratory, body composition.*

SKILL 3.3   Human biology: anatomy and physiology, including identification of major muscles, bones, and systems of the human body and their functions; exercise physiology, including terminology, components of fitness, principles of exercise, roles of body systems in exercise, short- and long-term effects of physical training, relationship between nutrition and fitness

MAJOR MUSCLES AND BONES; RELEVANT EXERCISES

Muscles

Shoulder
    Deltoids – Military/Shoulder Press

Arms
    Biceps Brachii – Front of upper arm - Curls
    Triceps Brachii – Back of upper arm - Triceps Extension

Legs
    Quadriceps – Front of upper leg – Leg Extensions
    Hamstrings – Back of upper leg – Leg Curls
    Gastrocnemius – Back of lower leg (calves) – Calf Raises
    Gluteus Maximus – Buttocks – Squats

Chest
    Pectoralis Major – Bench Press

Back
    Latissimus Dorsi – Chin-ups, Pull-ups

Waist
    Rectus Abdominis – Stomach/Abdominals – Sit-ups

Bones

Skull – comprised of cranium (head) and facial bones

Vertebral column – backbone
- seven cervical vertebrae (neck)
- twelve thoracic vertebrae (middle back)
- five lumbar vertebrae (lower back)

Shoulder
    Clavicle – Collarbone
    Scapula – Shoulder socket located on this bone

Thorax
    Sternum – breastbone
    Ribs – twelve pairs, each attaching to the twelve thoracic vertebrae

Arm
    Humerus – upper arm; attaches to scapula to form shoulder joint
    Ulna and Radius – forearm

Legs
    Femur – upper leg; largest bone in body
    Tibia and Fibula – lower leg
    Patella – knee

Hip
    Ilium, Ischium, and Pubis

STRUCTURES, LOCATIONS, AND FUNCTIONS OF THE THREE TYPES OF MUSCULAR TISSUE

The main function of the muscular system is movement. There are three types of muscle tissue: skeletal, cardiac, and smooth.

Skeletal muscle is voluntary. These muscles are attached to bones and are responsible for their movement. Skeletal muscle consists of long fibers and is striated due to the repeating patterns of the myofilaments (made of the proteins actin and myosin) that make up the fibers.

Cardiac muscle is found in the heart. Cardiac muscle is striated like skeletal muscle. It differs from skeletal muscle in that the plasma membrane of the cardiac muscle causes the muscle to beat even when away from the heart. The action potentials of cardiac and skeletal muscles also differ.

Smooth muscle is involuntary. It is found in organs and enables functions such as digestion and respiration. Unlike skeletal and cardiac muscle, smooth muscle is not striated. Smooth muscle has less myosin and does not generate as much tension as skeletal muscle.

MECHANISM OF SKELETAL MUSCLE CONTRACTION

A nerve impulse strikes a muscle fiber. This causes calcium ions to flood the sarcomere. Calcium ions allow ATP to expend energy. The myosin fibers creep along the actin, causing the muscle to contract. Once the nerve impulse has passed, calcium is pumped out and the contraction ends.

MOVEMENT OF BODY JOINTS

The axial skeleton consists of the bones of the skull and vertebrae. The appendicular skeleton consists of the bones of the legs, arms and tail, and shoulder girdle. Bone is a connective tissue. Parts of the bone include compact bone that gives strength, spongy bone that contains red marrow to make blood cells and yellow marrow in the center of long bones to store fat cells, and the periosteum that is the protective covering on the outside of the bone.

A joint is a place where two bones meet. Joints enable movement. Ligaments attach bone to bone. Tendons attach bone to muscle. Joints allow great flexibility in movement. There are three types of joints:

1. Ball and socket – allows for rotational movement. An example is the joint between the shoulder and the humerus. Ball and socket joints allow humans to move their arms and legs in different ways.

2. Hinge – movement is restricted to a single plane. An example is the joint between the humerus and the ulna.

3. Pivot – allows for the rotation of the forearm at the elbow and the hands at the wrist.

BODY SYSTEMS

MUSCULAR SYSTEM

The function of the muscular system is to provide optimal movement for the parts of the human body. The specific functions of each muscle depend on its location. In all cases, however, muscle action is the result of the action of individual muscle cells. Muscle cells are unique in that they are the only cells in the body that have the property of contractility. This gives muscle cells the ability to shorten and develop tension. This is extremely important for human movement.

Muscles are classified in three categories:

1. Skeletal: muscles that attach to the bone
2. Visceral: muscles that are associated with an internal body structure
3. Cardiac: muscles that form the wall of the heart

Skeletal muscles are the only voluntary muscles, meaning they contract as initiated by the will of a person.
Visceral and cardiac muscles are both involuntary muscles, meaning they are governed by nerve impulses found in the autonomic nervous system.

Skeletal and cardiac muscles are striated or band-like, whereas visceral muscles are smooth.

SKELETAL SYSTEM

The skeletal system has several functions:

1. Support: The skeleton acts as the framework of the body. It gives support to the soft tissues and provides points of attachment for the majority of the muscles.
2. Movement: The fact that the majority of the muscles attach to the skeleton and that many of the bones meet (or articulate) in moveable joints, the skeleton plays an important role in determining the extent and kind of movement that the body is capable of.
3. Protection: Clearly, the skeleton protects many of the vital, internal organs from injury. This includes the brain, spinal cord, thoracic, urinary bladder and reproductive organs.
4. Mineral Reservoir: Vital minerals are stored in the bones of the skeleton. Some examples are calcium, phosphorus, sodium and potassium.
5. Hemopoiesis or blood-cell formation: After a mother gives birth, the red marrow in specific bones produces the blood cells found in the circulatory system.

The human skeletal is composed of 206 individual bones that are held in position by strong fibrous ligaments. These bones can be grouped into two categories:

1. Axial skeleton: total 80 bones (skull, vertebral column, thorax)
2. Appendicular skeleton: total 126 bones (pectoral, upper limbs, pelvic, lower limbs)

The ENDOCRINE SYSTEM

The endocrine system is not a clearly defined anatomical system but rather is composed of various glands that are located throughout the body. The main function of this system is to aid in the regulation of body activities by producing chemical substances we know as hormones. Through a complicated regulation system, the bloodstream distributes hormones throughout the body with each hormone affecting only specific targeted organs.

The primary endocrine glands are the pituitary, thyroid, parathyroids, adrenals, pancreas and gonads. Additionally, the kidneys, gastrointestinal and placenta exhibit endocrine activity but to a lesser extent than the primary glands.

The hormones produced by the endocrine system do not fall into an easily defined class of chemical substances. Some are steroids (such as cortisol), others are proteins (such as insulin), and still others are polypeptides and amino acids (such as parathyroid hormone and epinephrine).

Regardless of the specific chemical substance, the hormones produced by the endocrine system play a critical role in aiding the regulation and integration of the body processes.

IMMUNE SYSTEM

The immune system's function is to defend the human body against infectious organisms and other attacking forces, such as bacteria, microbes, viruses, toxins and parasites. Simply put, the immune system strives every day to keep human beings healthy and free of disease and illness.

The immune system is made up of two main fluid systems - the blood stream and the lymph system. They are intertwined throughout the body and are responsible for transporting the agents of the immune system. White blood cells are considered to be the most important part of your immune system.
Different types/names of white blood cells are:
- Leukocytes – this is often used as the primary term for white blood cells
- Lymphocyte
- Monocytes
- Granulocytes
- B-cells
- Plasma cells
- T-cells
- Helper T-cells
- Killer T-cells
- Suppressor T-cells
- Natural killer cells
- Neutrophils

- Eosinophils
- Basophils
- Phagocytes
- Macrophages

A foreign substance that invades the body is referred to as an antigen. When an antigen is detected, the immune system goes into action immediately. Several types of cells start working together. These initial cells try to recognize and respond to the antigen, thereby triggering white blood cells to release antibodies. Antigens and antibodies have been referred to as fitting like a "key and a lock" throughout the scientific community. Once these antigens have been produced in the body they stay in the body. If this same antigen enters the body again, the body is immune and protected.

Vaccines are antigens given in very small amounts. They stimulate both humoral and cell mediated responses. After vaccination, memory cells recognize future exposure to the antigen so the body can produce antibodies much faster.

There are three types of immunity:

1. Innate Immunity: the immunity (general protection) we are all born with
2. Adaptive Immunity: immunity that develops throughout our lives (antibodies) as we are exposed to diseases and illnesses
3. Passive Immunity: this is an immunity that comes from outside us (outside antibiotics…)

There are two defense mechanisms in the immune system: non-specific and specific.

The **non-specific** immune mechanism has two lines of defense. The first line of defense is the physical barriers of the body. These include the skin and mucous membranes. The skin prevents the penetration of bacteria and viruses as long as there are no abrasions on the skin. Mucous membranes form a protective barrier around the digestive, respiratory, and genitourinary tracts. In addition, the pH of the skin and mucous membranes inhibit the growth of many microbes. Mucous secretions (tears and saliva) wash away many microbes and contain lysozyme that kills microbes.

The second line of defense includes white blood cells and the inflammatory response. **Phagocytosis** is the ingestion of foreign particles. Neutrophils make up about seventy percent of all white blood cells. Monocytes mature to become macrophages, which are the largest phagocytic cells. Eosinophils are also phagocytic. Natural killer cells destroy the body's own infected cells instead of invading the microbe directly.

The other second line of defense is the inflammatory response. The blood supply to the injured area increases, causing redness and heat. Swelling also typically occurs with inflammation. Basophils and mast cells release histamine in response to cell injury. This triggers the inflammatory response.

The **specific** immune mechanism recognizes specific foreign material and responds by destroying the invader. These mechanisms are specific and diverse. They are able to recognize individual pathogens.

CIRCULATORY SYSTEM

The function of the closed circulatory system (**cardiovascular system**) is to carry oxygenated blood and nutrients to all cells of the body and return carbon dioxide waste to the lungs for expulsion. Or paraphrased the function of the circulatory system is to transport blood leaving the heart to all parts of the body, permitting the exchange of certain substances between the blood and body fluids and ultimately returning the blood to the heart.

The circulatory system is composed of veins, arteries and capillaries. Arteries carry blood away from the heart, veins return blood to the heart and capillaries allow for the exchange of substances between the blood and the cells of the body. Capillaries are the most important vessels of the blood vascular system. Arteries must be able to withstand great pressure and veins are the largest vessels of the system.

The heart, blood vessels, and blood make up the cardiovascular system, which is closely related to the circulatory system.

The following diagram shows the structure of the heart, noting the specific arteries and veins:

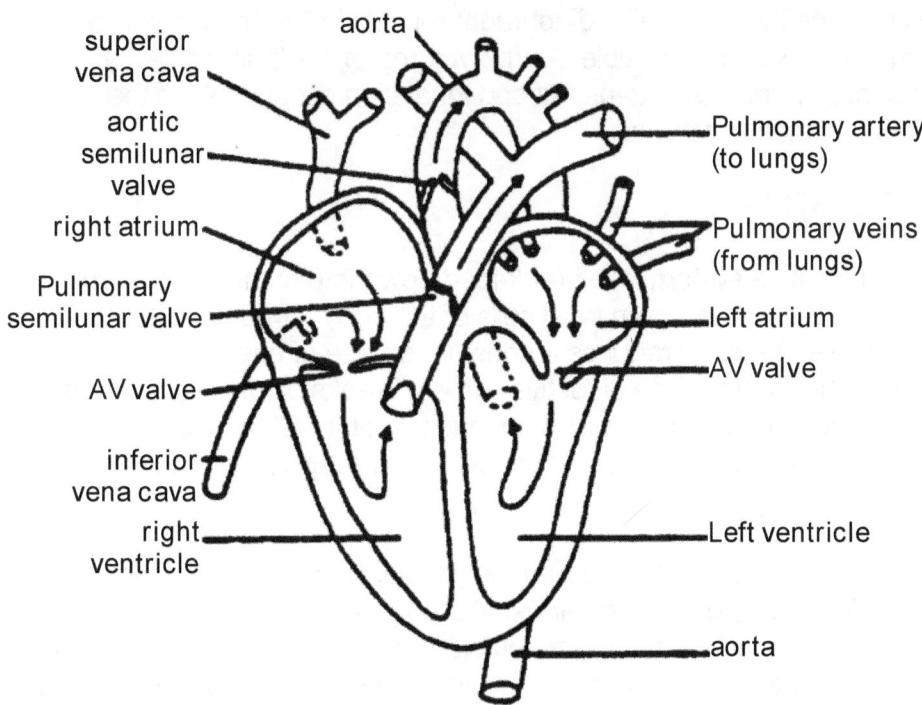

THE RESPIRATORY SYSTEM

The primary function of the respiratory system is the intake of oxygen brought into the body through normal breathing or aerobic activity and removal of carbon dioxide with the assistance of the circulatory system. The respiratory system also makes vocalization possible. We are able to speak, sing and laugh by varying the tension of the vocal cords as exhaled air passes over them.

The lungs are the respiratory surface of the human respiratory system. A dense net of capillaries contained just beneath the epithelium form the respiratory surface. The surface area of the epithelium is about $100m^2$ in humans. The volume of air inhaled and exhaled is the tidal volume. This is normally about 500mL in adults. Vital capacity is the maximum volume the lungs can inhale and exhale. This is usually around 3400mL.

To describe the respiratory system more thoroughly, air enters the mouth and nose, where it is warmed, moistened and filtered of dust and particles. Cilia in the trachea trap and expel unwanted material in the mucus. The trachea splits into two bronchial tubes and the bronchial tubes divide into smaller and smaller bronchioles in the lungs. The internal surface of the lung is composed of alveoli, which are thin walled air sacs. These allow for a large surface area for gas exchange. Capillaries line the alveoli. Oxygen diffuses into the bloodstream and carbon dioxide diffuses out of the capillaries and is exhaled from the lungs due to partial pressure. Hemoglobin, a protein containing iron, carries the oxygenated blood to the heart and all parts of the body.

The thoracic cavity holds the lungs. The diaphragm muscle below the lungs is an adaptation that makes inhalation possible. As the volume of the thoracic cavity increases, the diaphragm muscle flattens out and inhalation occurs. When the diaphragm relaxes, exhalation occurs.

THE DIGESTIVE SYSTEM

The function of the digestive system is to break food down into nutrients, absorb them into the blood stream, and deliver them to all cells of the body for use in cellular respiration. Every cell in the body requires a constant source of energy in order to perform its particular function(s). The digestive system breaks down or alters ingested food by mechanical and chemical processes so that it can ultimately cross the wall of the gastrointestinal tract and enter the blood vascular and lymphatic (circulatory) systems.

The digestive system consists of a tube called the gastrointestinal tract (alimentary canal) that extends from the mouth to the anus. As long as food remains in the gastrointestinal tract it is considered to still be outside the body. To "enter" the body, it must cross the wall of the digestive tract. Emptying into the digestive tube are the secretions of the salivary glands, gastric glands, intestinal glands, liver and pancreas, all of which assist in the digestion of food. These regions include the mouth, esophagus, stomach, small and large intestines.

Activities of the digestive system can be divided into six parts:

1. ingestion of food into the mouth
2. movement of food along the digestive tract
3. mechanical preparation of food for digestion
4. chemical digestion of food
5. absorption of digested food into the circulatory and lymphatic systems (circulatory system)
6. elimination of indigestible substances and waste products from the body by defecation

REPRODUCTIVE SYSTEM

The reproductive system differs greatly from the other organ systems of the body in that it does not contribute to the survival or homeostasis of a human being. Instead, the organs of the reproductive system ensure the continuance of the species.

The reproductive system produces gametes (germ cells). Through sexual intercourse, the male gamete (sperm) joins with a female gamete (ovum). This joining is called fertilization. The organs of the female reproductive system provide a suitable environment in which the fertilized ovum (zygote) can develop into a stage in which it is capable of surviving outside of the mother's body.

The organs that produce the gametes are referred to as the primary or essential sex organs. Specifically, these are the gonads (testes) in the male and the ovaries in the female. Additionally, the organs that produce the gametes are also responsible for producing hormones that influence the development of secondary sex characteristics and regulation of the reproductive system. In the male, specialized cells in the testes produce androgen hormones. The most active of these is testosterone. In the female, the ovaries produce estrogen and progesterone.

The structures that transport, protect and nourish the gametes in both the male and female are referred to as accessory sex organs. In the male, these include:

- the epididymis
- the ductus deferens
- the seminal vesicles
- the prostate gland
- the scrotum
- the penis

Female accessory sex organs include:

- the uterine tubes
- the uterus
- the vagina
- the vulva

NUTRITION AND WEIGHT CONTROL

Identify the components of nutrition

The components of nutrition are **carbohydrates, proteins, fats, vitamins, minerals, and water.**

Carbohydrates – the main source of energy (glucose) in the human diet. The two types of carbohydrates are simple and complex. Complex carbohydrates have greater nutritional value because they take longer to digest, contain dietary fiber, and do not excessively elevate blood sugar levels. Common sources of carbohydrates are fruits, vegetables, grains, dairy products, and legumes.

Proteins – are necessary for growth, development, and cellular function. The body breaks down consumed protein into component amino acids for future use. Major sources of protein are meat, poultry, fish, legumes, eggs, dairy products, grains, and legumes.

Fats – a concentrated energy source and important component of the human body. The different types of fats are saturated, monounsaturated, and polyunsaturated. Polyunsaturated fats are the healthiest because they may lower cholesterol levels, while saturated fats increase cholesterol levels. Common sources of saturated fats include dairy products, meat, coconut oil, and palm oil. Common sources of unsaturated fats include nuts, most vegetable oils, and fish.

Vitamins and minerals – organic substances that the body requires in small quantities for proper functioning. People acquire vitamins and minerals from their diets and from supplements. Important vitamins include A, B, C, D, E, and K. Important minerals include calcium, phosphorus, magnesium, potassium, sodium, chlorine, and sulfur.

Water – makes up 55 – 75% of the human body. It is essential for most bodily functions and is attained through food and liquids.

Determine the adequacy of diets in meeting the nutritional needs of students

Nutritional requirements *vary from person-to-person.* General guidelines for meeting adequate nutritional needs are: *no more than 30% total caloric intake from fats* (preferably 10% from saturated fats, 10% from monounsaturated fats, 10% from polyunsaturated fats), *no more than 15% total caloric intake from protein* (complete), *and at least 55% of caloric intake from carbohydrates* (mainly complex carbohydrates).

Exercise and diet help maintain proper body weight by equalizing caloric intake and caloric output.

Determine the role of exercise and diet in the maintenance of proper weight management

Nutrition and exercise are closely related concepts important to student health. An important responsibility of physical education instructors is to teach students proper nutrition and exercise and how they relate to each other. The two key components of a healthy lifestyle are consumption of a balanced diet and regular physical activity. Nutrition can affect physical performance. Proper nutrition produces high energy levels and allows for peak performance. Inadequate or improper nutrition can impair physical performance and lead to short-term and long-term health problems (e.g. depressed immune system and heart disease, respectively). Regular exercise improves overall health. Benefits of regular exercise include a stronger immune system, stronger muscles, bones, and joints, reduced risk of premature death, reduced risk of heart disease, improved psychological well-being, and weight management.

Recognize fallacies and dangers underlying selected diet plans

High Carbohydrate diets (i.e. Pritikin, Bloomingdale's) can produce rapid or gradual weight loss, depending on caloric intake. Vitamin and mineral supplements are usually needed because protein intake is low. These diets may or may not recommend exercising or permanent lifestyle changes, which are necessary to maintain one's weight.

High-Protein Diets promote the same myths, fallacies, and results as high carbohydrate diets. High-protein diets also require vitamin and mineral supplements. In addition, these diets are usually high in saturated fats and cholesterol because of the emphasis on meat products.

Liquid Formulas that are physician/hospital run (i.e. Medifast, Optifast) provide 800 or fewer calories a day consumed in liquid form. Dieters forgo food intake for 12 to 16 weeks in lieu of the protein supplement. Liquid diets require vitamin and mineral supplements and close medical supervision. Food is gradually reintroduced after the initial fast.

These diets can result in severe and/or dangerous metabolic problems in addition to an irregular heartbeat, kidney infections and failure, hair loss, and sensations of feeling cold and/or cold intolerance. These diets are very expensive and have a high rate of failure.

Over-The-Counter Liquid Diets (i.e. Slimfast) are liquid/food bar supplements taken in place of one or more meals per day. Such diets advocate an intake of 1,000 calories daily. Carbohydrate, protein, vitamin, and mineral intake may be so low that the diet can be as dangerous as the medically supervised liquid diets when relied on as the only source of nutrition. Because of the lack of medical supervision, the side effects can be even more dangerous.

Over-The-Counter Diet Pills/Aids and Prescription Diet Pills (appetite suppressants) have as their main ingredient phenyl propanolamine hydrochloride [PPA]. Keeping weight off by the use of these products is difficult. Dizziness, sleeplessness, high blood pressure, palpitation, headaches, and tachycardia are potential side effects of these products. Moreover, prescription diet pills can be addictive.

Low Calorie Diets (caloric restricted) are the most misunderstood method of weight loss. However, restricting the intake of calories is the way most people choose to lose weight. All the focus is on food, creating anxiety over the restriction of food - especially favorite foods. These diets are also difficult to maintain and have a high failure rate. Like the other diets, once the diet is over, dieters regain weight quickly because they fail to make permanent behavioral changes. Side effects of caloric restriction include diarrhea, constipation, Ketosis, a lower basal metabolic rate, blood-sugar imbalances, loss of lean body tissue, fatigue, weakness, and emotional problems. Dietary supplements are needed.

Those who choose **fasting** (complete caloric restriction) to lose weight can deplete enough of the body's energy stores to cause death.

BENEFITS OF EXERCISE

Identify the physiological, psychological, and sociological benefits of fitness training

Physiological benefits of physical activity include:

- improved cardio-respiratory fitness
- improved muscle strength
- improved muscle endurance
- improved flexibility
- more lean muscle mass and less body fat
- quicker rate of recovery
- improved ability of the body to utilize oxygen
- lower resting heart rate
- increased cardiac output
- improved venous return and peripheral circulation
- reduced risk of musculoskeletal injuries
- lower cholesterol levels
- increased bone mass
- cardiac hypertrophy and size and strength of blood vessels
- increased number of red cells
- improved blood-sugar regulation
- improved efficiency of thyroid gland
- improved energy regulation
- increased life expectancy

EXERCISES THAT BENEFIT THE MAJOR MUSCLE GROUPS OF THE BODY

Some of the major muscle groups of the body important to physical fitness are the traps, delts, pecs, lats, obliques, abs, biceps, quadriceps, hamstrings, adductors, triceps, biceps, and gluts.

Dumbbell Shoulder Shrug
(Trapezius)

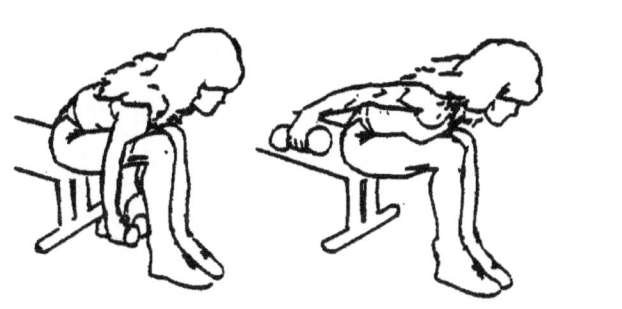

Seated Bent-Over Rear Deltoid Raise
(Rear Deltoids)

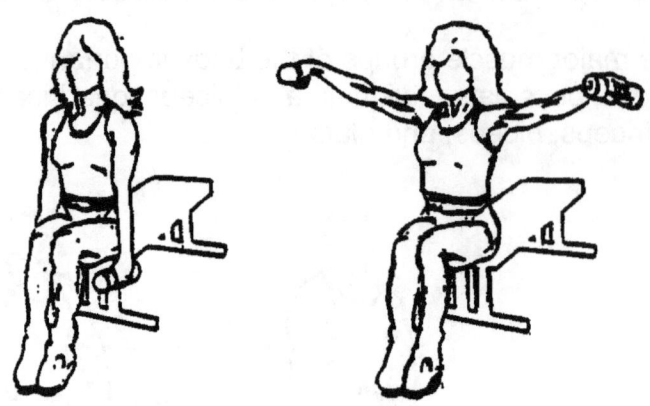

Seated Side Lateral Raise
(Front and Outer Deltoids)

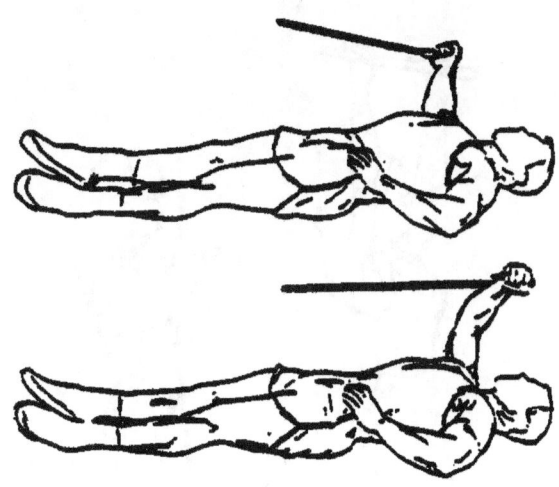

Lying Low-Pulley One-Arm Chest
(Lateral Pectorals)

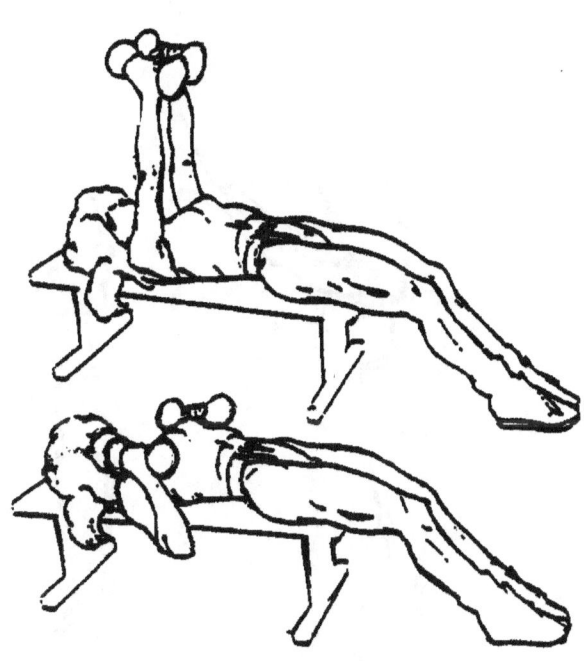

Flat Dumbbell Press
(Pectorals)

Medium-Grip Front-to-Rear Lat Pull Down
(Lats)

Straight-Arm Close-Grip Lat Pull Down
(Lats)

TEACHER CERTIFICATION STUDY GUIDE

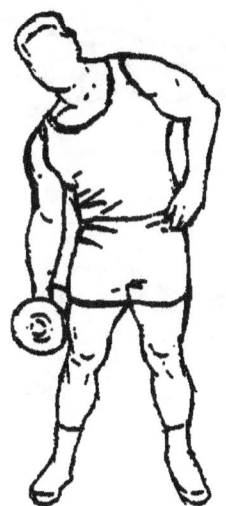

Dumbbell Side Bend
(Obliques)

Seated Barbell Twist
(Obliques)

PHYSICAL EDUCATION

TEACHER CERTIFICATION STUDY GUIDE

Leg Pull-In
(Lower Abdominals)

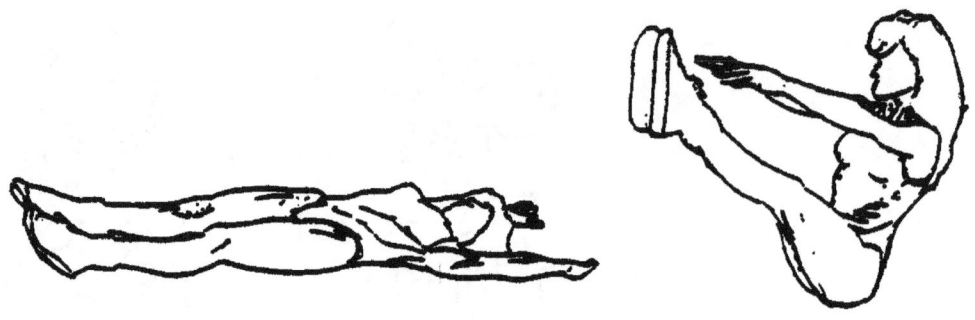

Jackknife Sit-Up
(Upper and Lower Abdominals)

Standing Alternated Dumbbell Curl
(Biceps)

Standing Medium-Grip Barbell Curl
(Biceps)

Standing Close-Grip Easy-Curl-Bar Triceps Curl
(Triceps)

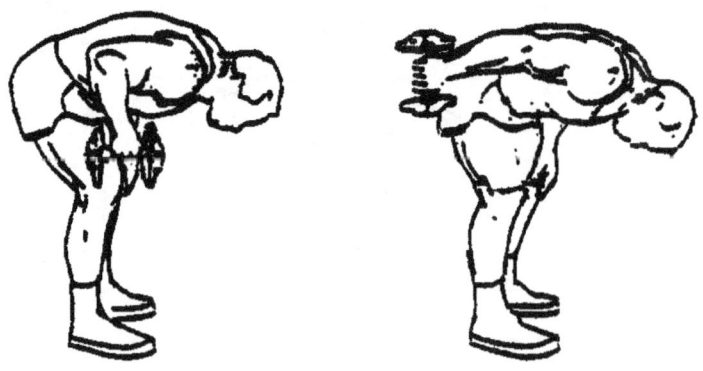

Standing Bent-Over One-Arm-Dumbbell Triceps Extension
(Triceps)

Flat-Footed Medium-Stance Barbell Half-Squat
(Thighs)

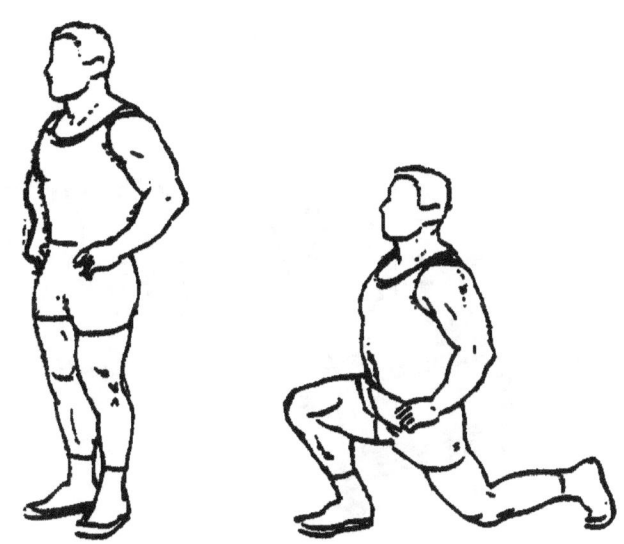

Freehand Front Lunge
(Thighs and Hamstrings)

TEACHER CERTIFICATION STUDY GUIDE

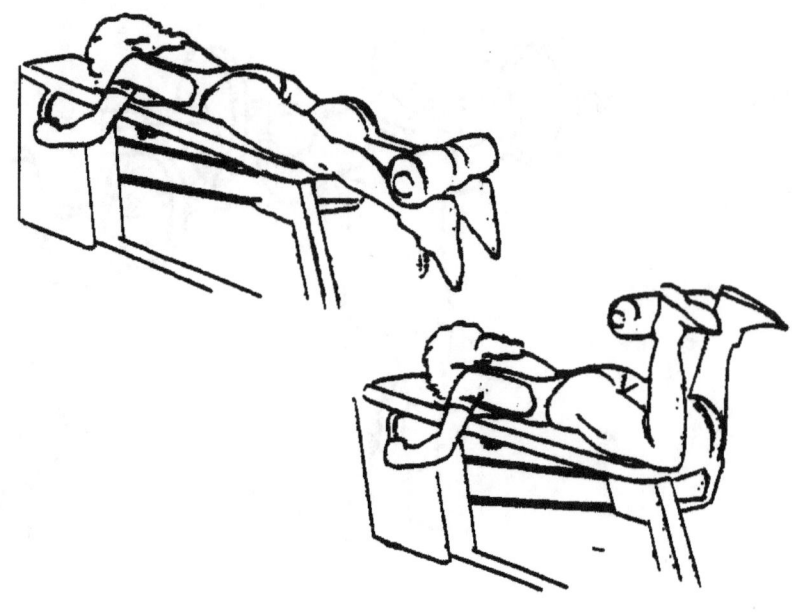

Thigh Curl on Leg Extension Machine
(Hamstrings)

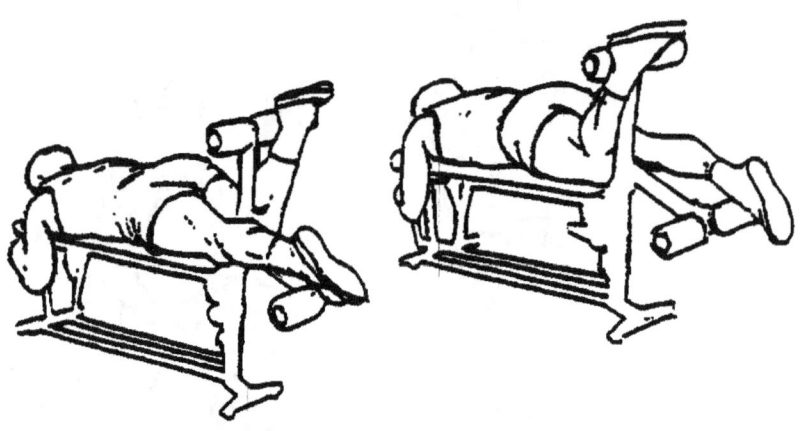

One-at-a-Time Thigh Curl on Leg Extension Machine
(Hamstings)

PHYSICAL EDUCATION 78

Hip Abduction
(Hips)

Hip Adduction
(Inner Thigh)

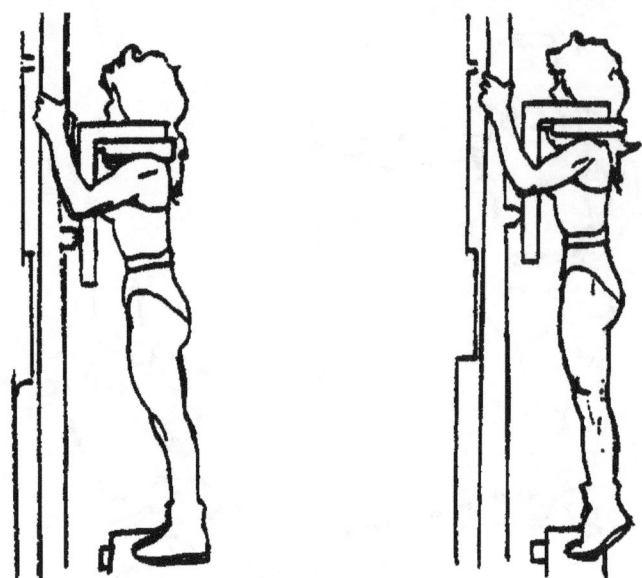

Standing Toe Raise on Wall Calf Machine
(Main Calf Muscles)

Standing Barbell Toe Raise
(Main Calf Muscles)

Hip Extension
(Hips and Thighs)

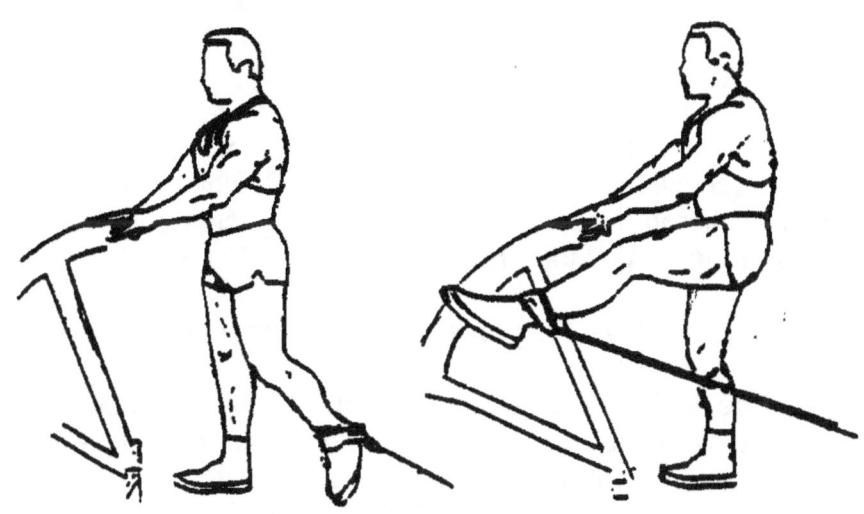

Hip Flexion
(Hip Flexors)

Identify diseases and conditions caused in part by a lack of physical activity

Hypertension, atherosclerosis, arteriosclerosis, heart attack, stroke, congestive heart failure, angina, osteoporosis, osteoarthritis, adult on-set diabetes, gout, gall bladder disorders, ulcers, cancer, lordosis, poor posture, neck, leg, knee, and foot problems are all diseases and conditions caused in part by a lack of physical activity.

Identify how the structure and function of the human body and its systems adapt to physical activity

The structure and function of the human body adapts greatly to physical activity and exertion. When challenged with any physical task, the human body responds through a series of integrated changes in function that involve most, if not all, of its physiological systems. Movement requires activation and control of the musculoskeletal system. The cardiovascular and respiratory systems provide the ability to sustain this movement over extended periods. When the body engages in exercise training several times, each of these physiological systems undergoes specific adaptations that increase the body's efficiency and capacity.

When the body works, it makes great demand on every muscle of the body. Either the muscles have to 'shut down' or they have to do work. The heart beats faster during strenuous exercise so that it can pump more blood to the muscles. The stomach shuts down during strenuous exercise so that it does not waste energy that the muscles need. Exercising makes the muscles work like motor that use up energy in order to generate force. Muscles, also known as 'biochemical motors', use the chemical adenosine triphosphate (ATP) as an energy source.

Different types of systems, such as the glycogen-lactic acid system, help muscles perform. Such systems help in producing ATP, which is extremely vital for working muscles. Aerobic respiration uses the fatty acids from fat reserves in muscle and helps produce ATP for a much longer period of time.

The following points summarize the process of bodily adaptation to exercise:

• Muscle cells use the ATP they have floating around in about 3 seconds.
• The phosphagen system kicks in and supplies energy for 8 to 10 seconds.
• If exercise continues longer, the glycogen-lactic acid system kicks in.
• Finally, if exercise continues, aerobic respiration takes over. This would occur in endurance events such as an 800-meter dash, marathon run, rowing, cross-country skiing, or distance skating.

Physical activity affects the cardiovascular and musculoskeletal systems the most. However, it also helps in proper functioning of metabolic, endocrine, and immune systems.

COMPETENCY 4.0 SOCIAL SCIENCE FOUNDATIONS

SKILL 4.1 History of physical education: leading men and women, major issues, and events; historical relationship of physical education to health and fitness

Germany, Sweden and England greatly influenced the early development of Physical Education, particularly from the late 1700's to the mid 1800's. Turner Societies were introduced to the states by German immigrants. Turner Societies advocated a system of gymnastics training that employed or utilized heavy equipment (e.g., horizontal and parallel bars, side horse) in their strife for fitness. In contrast, the Swedish preferred attaining and maintaining fitness through the use of light equipment. Their system of exercise to promote health was through systematic movements through the use of light equipment (e.g., ropes, climbing and wands). The English brought to America, sports and games. The type of sports and games that the English brought emphasized moral development through participation in physical activities.

In 1823, the first school to include physical education as a requirement in its curriculum was The Round Hill School, a private school in Northhampton, Massachusetts. After this and continuing throughout the 1800's, the inclusion of physical education in schools across America became prominent. The "first American to design a program of exercise for American children" was in 1824 by Catherine Beecher (Lumpkin, Angela. 1994. *Physical Education and Sport: A contemporary Introduction*, 3rd edition. St. Louis: Mosby. pg. 202). Ms. Beecher was the founder of the Hartford Female Seminary. The curriculum of physical education that Ms. Beecher designed consisted of what we would refer to today as calisthenics. She was also an extremely active advocate for including physical education into the public schools curriculum. It took until 1855 for this to happen, when Cincinnati, Ohio became the first city school system to offer physical education to its students in public schools.

California became the first state to pass a law, in 1866, that actually required two periods a day of exercise in its public schools. During this time, specifically between 1855 and 1900, Ms. Beecher, along with her contemporaries, Edward Hitchcock, Dudley Allen Sargent and Dio Lewis were the early leaders in physical education. Debates abounded as to whether it was best to use the system they had established in America or would it be better to use the Germans, Swedes or English systems as a way of providing a national physical education program for America. These debates were referred to as the *Battle of Systems*.

Throughout the 1890's and during this great period of debate, John Dewey challenged the traditional education system. Mr. Dewey and his colleagues were responsible for expanding the education system based on the "three R's", to include physical education in America. It was also during this time in history that many higher education schools began to offer training for physical education teachers. Because of the strong emphasis on the sciences, including courses in physiology and anatomy, many professors of these students held medical degrees.

In 1983, Thomas Wood stated that "the great thought of physical education is not the education of the physical nature, but the relation of physical training to complete education, and then the effort to make the physical training contribute its full share to the life of the individual." (National Education Association. 1893. *NEA Proceedings* 32:621. pg.621.) This was the beginning of a change in thinking with relation to the importance of physical education in regard to the overall education of the country's children. Many early twentieth century educational psychologists, including John Dewey, Edward Thorndike and Stanley Hall, supported Wood's line of thinking and the important role of children's play in furthering their ability to learn. As a result, in 1927, *The New Physical Education* was published by Wood and Rosalind Cassidy, who also was a strong advocate of education through the physical.

Charles McCloy, supported Wood's and Cassidy's line of thinking and published work. He believed that physical education was more than just contributing to the overall well-being and learning of children. He held that physical education's primary objective was the development of skills as well as the maintenance of the body. It was an expanded view on Wood's and Cassidy's theories. The testing of motor skills was a significant part of McCloy's contribution to physical education. Additionally, his philosophy of testing motor skills paralleled with the scientific movement in education during this time period.

In the early 1920's many states passed legislation that required physical education in the schools. This trend continued until the 1950's when all states eventually required physical education in their schools. The curriculum of physical education changed as the events in the country occurred. For example, during World War II, the emphasis in physical education shifted from games to physical conditioning. In 1953, the President's Council on Physical Fitness was established when it was noted through the Kraus-Weber study that American children were far less fit than children in European countries. The council was established to assist the falling fitness levels of America's children and youth.

THE HISTORY OF PHYSICAL EDUCATION AS A PROFESSION

Contributions of early societies to the profession

Games often had a practical, educational aim like playing house. In addition, games such as gladiatorial games had political aims. Economic games included fishing and hunting. Families played board games. There were ceremonial reasons for games found in dances. Finally, ball games provided an opportunity for socialization.

Early society - The common activities performed in early societies included warlike games, chariot racing, boating and fishing, equestrian, hunting, music and dancing, boxing and wrestling, bow and arrow activities, dice, and knucklebones.

Egyptian - The common activities performed in Egypt were acrobatics, gymnastics, tug of war, hoop and kick games, ball and stick games, juggling, knife-throwing games of chance, board games, and guessing games (e.g. how many fingers are concealed).

Bronze Age - The activities performed during the Bronze Age (3000 to 1000 BC) were bullfights, dancing, boxing, hunting, archery, running, and board games.

Greek Age - The Greeks are best known for the Olympic Games. Their other contributions were the pentathlon, which included the jump, the discus, and the javelin. The Pankration was a combination of boxing and wrestling. The Greeks also played on seesaws, enjoyed swinging, hand guessing games, blind man's bluff, dice games (losers had to carry their partner's pick-a-back), and hoop and board games. There also were funeral games in The Iliad.

Romans - The Romans kept slaves and were advocates of "blood sports." Their philosophy was to die well. There were unemployment games. Roman baths were popular, as were ball games, stuffed feathers, pila trigonalis, follis, and balloon or bladder ball. The Capitoline games were held in 86 AD. These union guild athletes were paid for their activities, which included artificial fly-fishing. The games that were popular during this period were top spinning, odds and evens, riding a long stick, knucklebones, and hide and seek.

Chinese - The Chinese contributed the following: jujitsu, fighting cocks, dog racing, and football. In Korea, Japan, and China, children played with toys and lanterns. Common activities included: building snowmen, playing with dolls, making/playing with shadows, flying kites, and fighting kites. Children enjoyed rope walker toys, windmills, turnip lanterns, ring puzzles, and playing horse. Noblemen engaged in hopping, jumping, leapfrog, jump rope, seesaw, and drawing.

Major events in the history of physical education and the historical relationship of physical education to health and fitness

Egypt - Sport dancing among the nobility, physical skills among the masses, and physical training for wars.

Cretans - learned to swim.

Spartan and Greeks - emphasized severe physical training and NOT competitive sport.

Athenians - believed in the harmonious development of the body, mind and spirit.

Romans – The Romans established the **worth of physical education**. During the dark ages, children learned fitness and horsemanship. The squires learned how to become knights by boxing and fencing. Swimming was also popular. During the Renaissance, people developed the body for health reasons. The Romans **combined the physical and mental** aspects of exercise in their daily routines.

1349-1428 - Physical education was necessary for a person's total education and also as a means of recreation.

In **1546,** Martin Luther saw PE as a substitute for vice and evil.

Sweden - Ling in 1839 strove to make PE a **science.**

Colonial period - Religion denounced play. Pleasure was either banned or frowned upon.

The **National Period** began in 1823. Games and sports were available as after school activities. There was an introduction of **gymnastics and calisthenics.**

Civil War (1860) this period saw gymnastics and non-military use of PE. Physical Education became **organized.** PE became part of the school curriculum and held a respectable status among other subjects. **YMCA** was founded. Gulick was the Director of PE at NYC and Dudley Allen Sargent was teaching physical education at Harvard.

Great Depression of the 1930s - **Physical fitness movement.** Bowling was the number one activity. Dance, gymnastics and sports were popular. The Heisman Trophy was awarded in 1935. After WWII, outdoor pools were common for the average American.

Major trends since WWII influencing physical education

WWII - Selective Service examinations revealed the poor physical fitness condition of the country's youth. Thus, **physical education classes focused on physical conditioning.**

1942 - President Roosevelt established the **Division of Physical Fitness** run by John B. Kelly (who alerted Roosevelt about the poor fitness levels of the youth). This division was dissolved and **placed under the Federal Security Agency** [FSA] with numerous organizations **promoting fitness**. Under the FSA, Frank Lloyd was Chief of the Physical Fitness Division, William Hughs was Chief Consultant, and Dorothy LaSalle was head of the work for women and children. **After WWII ended, the eagerness for fitness waned.**

1953 - **Kraus-Webber tests** - Of the 4,264 USA participants, 57% failed a general muscular fitness test. Only 8.7% of Europeans failed. Again, John Kelly alerted the President (Eisenhower) of the **need for a fitness movement.** Eisenhower ordered a **special conference** that was held in **June 1956.**

1956 - AAHPERD Fitness Conference established the President's Council on Youth Fitness and a President's Citizens Advisory Committee on the Fitness of American Youth.

Modern dance gave way to the contemporary. Gymnastics had new equipment, including a higher balance beam, trampolines, and uneven parallel bars. The Swedish gymnastics boom was over, and ropes and ladders, wands, dumbbells, and Indian clubs were no longer fashionable. Core sports for boys were football, baseball, basketball, and track and field. Core sports for women were basketball and volleyball.

John Fitzgerald Kennedy changed the name of the President's Citizens Advisory Committee of Fitness of American Youth to the **President's Council on Physical Fitness.**

Lyndon Baines Johnson changed the name to **President's Council on Physical Fitness and Sports.**

1972 - **Passage of Title IX** of the Educational Amendments Act to ensure girls and women receive the same rights as boys and men for educational programs - including physical education and athletics

1970 to Present Trends - Preventative medicine, wellness, physical fitness, and education that is more scholarly, more specialized, and more applicable to all segments of population such as the elderly, handicapped persons, and those out of organizations (Non-School sports): AAU - mid 20th century controlled amateur sports; Little League; North American Baseball Association.

International Amateur Sports: Olympic Governing Committee.

Intercollegiate: National Collegiate Athletic Association (NCAA scholarship in 1954); National Association of Intercollegiate Athletics (NAIA); National Junior College Athletic Association (NJCAA).

Interscholastic Sports: National Federation of State High School Athletic Associations.

Organizations for Girls' and Women's Sports: Athletic and Recreation Federation of College Women (ARFCW); the Women's Board of the U.S. Olympic Committee; National Section of Women's Athletics (NSWA - promoted intercollegiate sports such as US Field Hockey and Women's International Bowling and established special committees). The Women's Division of NAAF merged its interests in the NSWA of AAHPERD changing its name to National Section for Girls and Women's Sports (NSGWS). **Mel Lockes, chairperson of NSGWS in 1956, was against intercollegiate athletics for women.** In 1957, NSGWS changed its name to Division of Girls and Women's Sports (DGWS), still a division of AAHPER. A lack of funds hurt DGWS.

SKILL 4.2   Current philosophical issues: purpose of physical education; relationship between teaching and coaching; accountability; roles, benefits, and effects of competition

The various philosophies of education greatly influence the goals and values of physical education. Important educational philosophies related to physical education are Idealism, Realism, Pragmatism, Naturalism, Existentialism, Humanism, and Eclecticism.

Idealism – The **mind**, developed through the acquisition of knowledge, is of highest importance. Values exist independent of individuals. Fitness and strength activities contribute to the development of one's personality. Horace Mann, Wadsworth, Kant, Plato, and Descartes were Idealists.

Realism – The physical world is **real.** A realist believes in the laws of nature, the scientific method, and mind and body harmony. Religion and philosophy co-exist. Physical fitness results in greater productivity, physical drills are important to the learning process, athletic programs lead to desired social behavior, and play and recreation help life adjustment. Aristotle was a realist.

Pragmatism – **Experience** is the key to life. Dynamic experience shapes individuals' truth. Education is child-centered. Varied activities present experiences that are more meaningful. Activities promote socializing. Problem-solving accomplishes learning. John Dewy and Charles Pierce were pragmatists.

Naturalism – This philosophy is materialistic. Things that actually exist are found only within the physical realm of nature. Nature is valuable. The individual is more important than society. Self-activities accomplish learning and activities are more than physical in nature. Naturalists promote play and discourage high levels of competition. Physical education takes a holistic approach.

Existentialism – The chief concern is **individualism.** Existentialists do not want the individual to conform to society. They promote freedom of choice and a variety of interests. Individuals need to have their own system of values. Playing develops creativity and the discovery of the "inner self." Sartre, Soren, and Kierkegaard were Existentialists.

Humanism and **Eclecticism** – These are the modern philosophies of physical education that most schools follow today. The Humanistic philosophy is based on development of individual talents and total fulfillment that encourages total involvement and participation in one's environment. Humanists encourage self-actualization and self-fulfillment. Curriculums based on the Humanistic approach are more student-centered. The Eclectic approach combines beliefs from different philosophies and does not resemble any single philosophy. When blended skillfully, the Eclectic approach affords a sound philosophy for an individual.

Philosophies of education applied to physical education goals

Physical/Organic Development Goal (Realism philosophy) – activities build physical power by strengthening the body's systems, resulting in the ability to sustain adaptive effort, shorten recovery time, and develop resistance to fatigue. The core values are individual health, greater activity, and better performance by an adequately developed and properly functioning body.

Motor/Neuromuscular Development Goal (Realism philosophy) – develops body awareness producing movement that is proficient, graceful, and aesthetic and uses as little energy as possible. Students develop as many skills as possible so their interests are wide and varied to allow more enjoyment and better adjustment to group situations. Varied motor development skills affect health by influencing how leisure time is spent. Values include reducing energy expenditure, building confidence, bringing recognition, enhancing physical and mental health, making participation safer, and contributing to aesthetic sense.

Cognitive Development Goal (Idealism philosophy) – deals with acquiring knowledge and ability to think and interpret knowledge. Scientific principles explain time, space, and flow of movement. Learning physical activities requires thinking and coordination of movements and mastering and adapting to one's environment. Individuals also should acquire knowledge of rules, techniques, and strategies of activities. Cognitive values include healthy attitudes and habits such as body awareness, personal hygiene, disease prevention, exercise, proper nutrition, and knowledge of health service providers.

Social/Emotional/Affective Development Goal (Existentialism philosophy) – deals with helping individuals make adjustments – personal, group, and societal – by positively influencing human behavior. Performance defines success, and success develops self-confidence. Wholesome attitude throughout the various growth stages promote the development of an appropriate self-concept, which is very important. Values include meeting basic social needs (sense of belonging, recognition, self-respect, and love) that produce a socially, well-adjusted individual.

RELATIONSHIP BETWEEN TEACHING AND COACHING

Teaching and athletic coaching share many similarities and a few key differences. Both teachers and coaches must be able to identify students' mistakes and deficiencies and devise plans that will produce improvement. In addition, teachers and coaches must work effectively with students of different personality types, ability levels, and learning styles. Finally, teachers and coaches must be able to communicate well with their students and develop a relationship of trust that produces a positive learning environment.

Teaching and athletic coaching differ in two important ways. First, while teaching is always a long-term process with long-term achievement goals, coaching may involve either a long-term or short-term coach-student relationship. For example, a beginning tennis player may desire a coach that will mold her game over many years (long-term relationship), while a more advanced player may seek a coach to help fix a particular stroke (short-term relationship). The second key difference is that coaching requires different motivational tactics. Athletic coaches must often convince students that they need to change a particular technique or strategy and motivate students through periods of skill regression when they implement changes. While teachers must motivate students to learn, they most likely do not have to sell students on a particular method of learning.

ACCOUNTABILITY

Accountability is a major issue in physical education. The declining status of physical education in school curricula is attributable, in part, to a lack of accountability for teachers, students, and schools. The importance placed on academic testing has caused schools to decrease the time spent on physical education. In addition, schools often fail to hold physical education instructors to the same achievement standards as academic teachers. Instructors often do not assess and monitor student progress and development in athletic skill and fitness. To regain its position as an important part of the learning environment, physical education must increase accountability. Well-trained and qualified instructors must implement lesson plans and assessments that help students develop skill and fitness. Instructors and school officials should base student assessments on personal progress, not generic achievement standards.

ROLES, BENEFITS, AND EFFECTS OF COMPETITION

Competition is the ultimate test of athletic skill, fitness, and performance. Competitive athletic events help assess a student's skill level, mental toughness, desire, and effort. Competition also provides many life lessons that benefits participants physically, personally, and socially.

The physical benefits of competitive sports are many. Participation in sports provides fitness maintenance, stress relief, satisfaction derived from mastering skills, and exposure to healthy lifestyle habits.

Competitive sports also teach life lessons that benefit participants on many personal levels. Competition demonstrates the value of preparation and hard work. In addition, participants learn teamwork, time management, and leadership skills. Finally, participants in competitive sports learn resilience from dealing with injuries, losses, setbacks, and adversity.

Competitive sports are also an excellent social activity. Participants build relationships, interact with others with similar interests, and learn to recognize the value of diversity.

While the effects of competition are largely positive, negative experiences in competitive sports can be very damaging. Overzealous coaches and parents, overly competitive and hostile teammates and opponents, and unnecessary pressure and expectations are common problems in youth athletics. Coaches, parents, and youth league officials must closely monitor competitive situations to ensure that all participants have a positive experience.

SKILL 4.3 Sociological and sociopolitical issues: cultural diversity, equity (Title IX, Individuals with Disabilities Education Act, affirmative action), general educational issues

SOCIOLOGICAL ASPECTS OF PHYSICAL EDUCATION

The role physical activity can play in developing an understanding of diversity and cultural differences among people

Physical activity and related games can introduce children to the concepts of equity and fairness. In addition, physical activity provides a venue for the interaction of diverse groups of people, allowing participants to observe and appreciate cultural differences and similarities.

- **Human Growth and Development** – Movement activities promote personal growth and development physically, by way of stimulating muscular development. They promote growth emotionally, by raising personal confidence levels among children and by allowing them to explore concepts of inter-group equity that may at first seem threatening. To the insecure child, the concept that another group may be equal to his own may seem to 'demote' his group and the child by extension.

- **Psychology** – Observation and interaction with children from diverse backgrounds in a training environment (where the training activities tend to focus more on 'doing', which feels more genuine to children than the classroom setting of raising hands and answering questions) allows the child to see in others the same sorts of behavioral reasoning processes that he sees in himself. This humanizes others from diverse backgrounds, and promotes the concept of equity among diverse groups.

- **Aesthetics** – Human movement activities create an opportunity for individual participation in activities with intrinsic aesthetic qualities. A gymnastic technique or a perfectly executed swing of a baseball bat relies on both physical training and a level of intuitive action. This is an artistic form of expression that is readily accessible to children. Recognizing beauty in the activities and performances of others (in some cases from groups different from that of the viewing student) is a humanizing experience.

Equity – Federal Legislation

The Department of Health and Human Services recommended legislative changes - including those for education. **Title IX** prohibits sex discrimination in educational programs. **PL 94-142** requires schools to provide educational services for handicapped students. In 1990, Congress passed the **Individuals with Disabilities Education Act** (IDEA) that amended earlier laws. IDEA specifies physical education as a required educational service. In addition, IDEA defines physical education as the development of physical fitness, motor skills, and skills in group and individual games and dance, aquatics, and lifetime sports.

Title IX takes precedence over all conflicting state and local laws and conference regulations. Federal aid (even aid not related to physical education or athletics) must comply with Title IX. Finally, Title IX prohibits discrimination in personnel standards and scholarships selection.

Equity – Affirmative Action

Affirmative action is an attempt to increase minority representation in higher education and the workplace. Minority representation in physical education and athletic coaching is particularly important because of the diversity in the student population. A major focus of affirmative action in physical education is increasing the number of minority students in higher education programs such as physical therapy, athletic training, and recreational management.

Social skills and values gained from participation in physical activities

- The ability to make adjustments to both self and others by an integration of the individual into society and the environment.

- The ability to make judgments in a group situation.

- Learning to communicate with others and cooperate.

- The development of the social phases of personality, attitudes, and values required to become a functioning member of society, such as consideration for others' feelings.

- The development of a sense of belonging and acceptance by society.

- The development of positive personality traits.

- Learning of constructive use of leisure time.

- A development of attitude that reflects good moral character.

- Respect for school rules and property.

Activities that enhance socialization

At the junior high level, students often have a desire to play on a team. They also emphasize that they want to learn activities that will prove useful in their leisure hours.

The senior high level students desire to play harmoniously with others and to participate in team play. Students view activities such as dance and sports as a time where they learn to respect their fellow students. The change of pace that physical education classes offer when compared to traditional academic classes provides opportunities for enhanced socialization.

Basketball, baseball, football, soccer, softball, and volleyball are social, team activities. Tennis and golf are social activities that are useful in leisure hours.

SKILL 4.4   Psychology: personality factors that affect participation, social-psychological factors that affect participation, cooperation

PERSONALITY FACTORS

Certain psychological aspects may hinder participation in certain physical activities. These factors can depend on the individual, the group the individual will participate with, and the activity itself.

An individual's personality type and interests can determine their level of participation. Outgoing, energetic, and aggressive personality types usually exhibit increased levels of participation. Reserved or lazy personality types are sometimes difficult to work with and motivate. Shy individuals are usually compliant, but may not feel completely comfortable in participation, especially in activities involving larger groups.

Physical education instructors often overlook the importance of activity groups for the psychological well-being of students. Instructors must construct groups with certain factors in mind. Children may feel intimidated by participating in activities with older individuals. In addition, girls may not feel comfortable participating with boys, and vice versa. Grouping students by age, gender, and skill level helps maintain self-confidence.

The type of activity can also affect participation. Every one has different interests and instructors should not necessarily force students to participate in activities they do not enjoy. Such action can lead to a diminished physical activity level throughout life. Instructors should introduce alternate activities to increase levels of participation for all individuals.

POSITIVE AND NEGATIVE INFLUENCES OF PARTICIPATION IN PHYSICAL ACTIVITY ON PSYCHO-SOCIAL FACTORS

Physical activity can influence psycho-social development both positively and negatively. Thus, physical education instructors must create an environment that maximizes the benefits of physical activity and minimizes the potential negative aspects.

Positive Individual Influences:

Reduces tension and depression; provides means of affiliation with others; provides exhilarating experiences; provides aesthetic experiences; creates positive body image; controls aggression, provides relaxation and a change of pace from long hours of work, study, or other stresses; provides challenge and sense of accomplishment; provides a way to be healthy and fit; improves self-esteem through skill mastery; provides creative experiences; creates positive addiction to exercise in contrast to negative addiction to substances.

Positive Group Influences:

Development of cooperation skills; acceptance of and respect for all persons regardless of race, creed or origin; assimilation of the group attitude; opportunity to develop group relationships; development of a spirit of fairness; development of traits of good citizenship; development of leadership and following skills; development of self-discipline; additional avenues for social acquaintances; development of social poise and self-understanding; development of a social consciousness with an accompanying sense of values; and individual and social development.

Negative influences:

Ego-centered athletes; winning at all costs; false values; harmful pressures; loss of identity; role conflict; aggression and violence; compulsiveness; over-competitiveness; addiction to exercise, where commitment to exercise has a higher priority than commitments to family, interpersonal relationships, work, and medical advice; escape or avoidance of problems; exacerbation of anorexia nervosa; exercise deprivation effects; fatigue; overexertion; poor eating habits; self-centeredness; preoccupation with fitness, diet, and body image.

COMPETENCY 5.0 BIOMECHANICS

SKILL 5.1 Terminology: mass, force, friction

Mass: 1. A grouping of individual parts or elements that compose a unified body of unspecified size or quantity. 2. The quantity of matter in a given object.

Force: The capacity to do work or cause physical change; energy, strength, or active power.

Friction: A force that resists the relative motion or tendency to such motion of two bodies in contact; rubbing of one object or surface against another.

SKILL 5.2 Basic principles of movement: summation of forces, center of gravity, force/speed relations, torque

KNOWLEDGE OF MECHANICAL PRINCIPLES OF BODY MANAGEMENT

Concepts of equilibrium and center of gravity applied to movement

Body mass redistributes when body segments move independently. This changes the location of the body's center of gravity. Segments also move to change the body's base of support from one moment to the next to cope with imminent loss of balance.

The entire center of gravity of the body shifts in the same direction of movement of the body's segments. As long as the center of gravity remains over the base of support, the body will remain in a state of equilibrium. The more the center of gravity is situated over the base, the greater the stability. A wider base of support and/or a lower center of gravity enhances stability. To be effective, the base of support must widen in the direction of the force produced or opposed by the body. Shifting weight in the direction of the force in conjunction with widening the base of support further enhances stability.

Constant interaction of forces that move the body in the elected direction results in dynamic balance. The smooth transition of the center of gravity changing from one base of support to the next produces speed.

Concept of force applied to movement

Force is any influence that can change the state of motion of an object; we must consider the objective of movement.

Magnitude of Force – force must overcome the inertia of the object and any other resisting forces for movement to occur.

For linear movement, force applied close to the center of gravity requires a smaller magnitude of force to move the object than does force applied farther from the center of gravity.

For rotational movement, force applied farther from the center of gravity requires a smaller magnitude of force to rotate the object than does force applied closer to the center of gravity.

For objects with a fixed point, force applied anywhere other than through the point of fixation results in object rotation.

Energy – the capacity to do work. (The more energy a body has the greater the force with which it can move something [or change its shape] and/or the farther it can move it).

Movement (mechanical energy) has two types:

1. Potential energy (energy possessed by virtue of position, absolute location in space or change in shape).

    A. Gravitational potential energy - potential energy of an object that is in a position where gravity can act on it.

    B. Elastic (strain) potential energy - energy potential of an object to do work while recoiling (or reforming) after stretching, compressing, or twisting.

2. Kinetic energy (energy possessed by virtue of motion that increases with speed).

Force Absorption - maintaining equilibrium while receiving a moving object's kinetic energy without sustaining injury or without losing balance while rebounding. The force of impact is dependent on an object's weight and speed. The more abruptly kinetic energy is lost, the more likely injury or rebound occurs. Thus, **absorbing force requires gradually decelerating a moving mass by utilization of smaller forces over a longer period of time**. Stability is greater when the force is received closer to the center of gravity.

Striking resistive surfaces - the force of impact per unit area decreases when the moving object's area of surface making contact increases and the surface area that the object strikes increases.

Striking non-resistive surfaces - the force of impact decreases if the moving object's area of surface making contact decreases because it is more likely to penetrate.

The more time and distance that it takes to stop a moving object when striking any surface, the more gradually the surface absorbs the force of impact. Also the reaction forces acting upon the moving object decrease.

Equilibrium returns easily when the moving body (striking a resistive surface) aligns the center of gravity more vertically over the base of support.

Angular force against a body decreases when the distance between a contacting object and the body decreases and the contact occurs closer to the center of gravity. Also, widening the base of support in the direction of the moving object will increase stability.

Concept of leverage applied to movement

First-class lever - the axis is between the points of application of the force and the resistance.

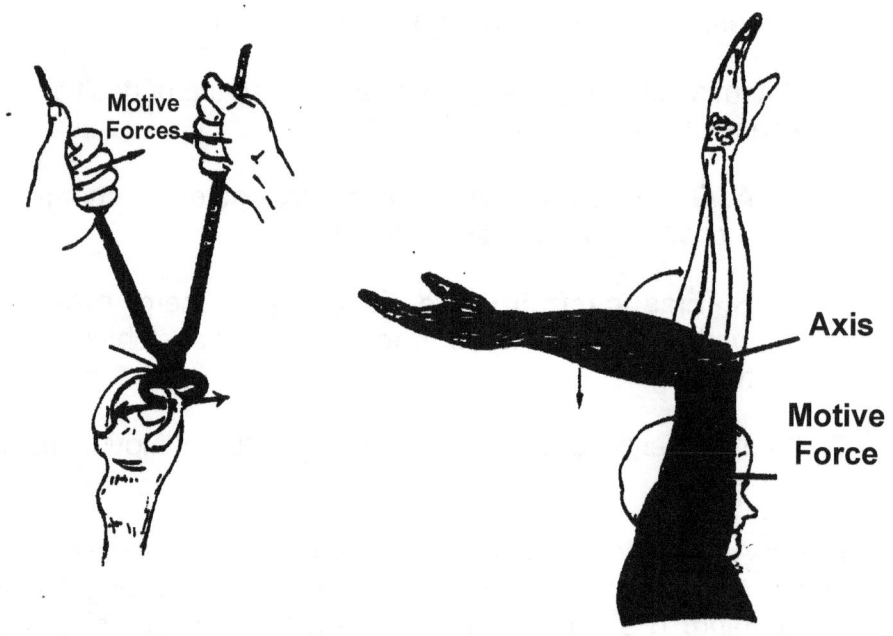

Second-class lever - the force arm is longer than the resistance arm (operator applies resistance between the axis and the point of application of force).

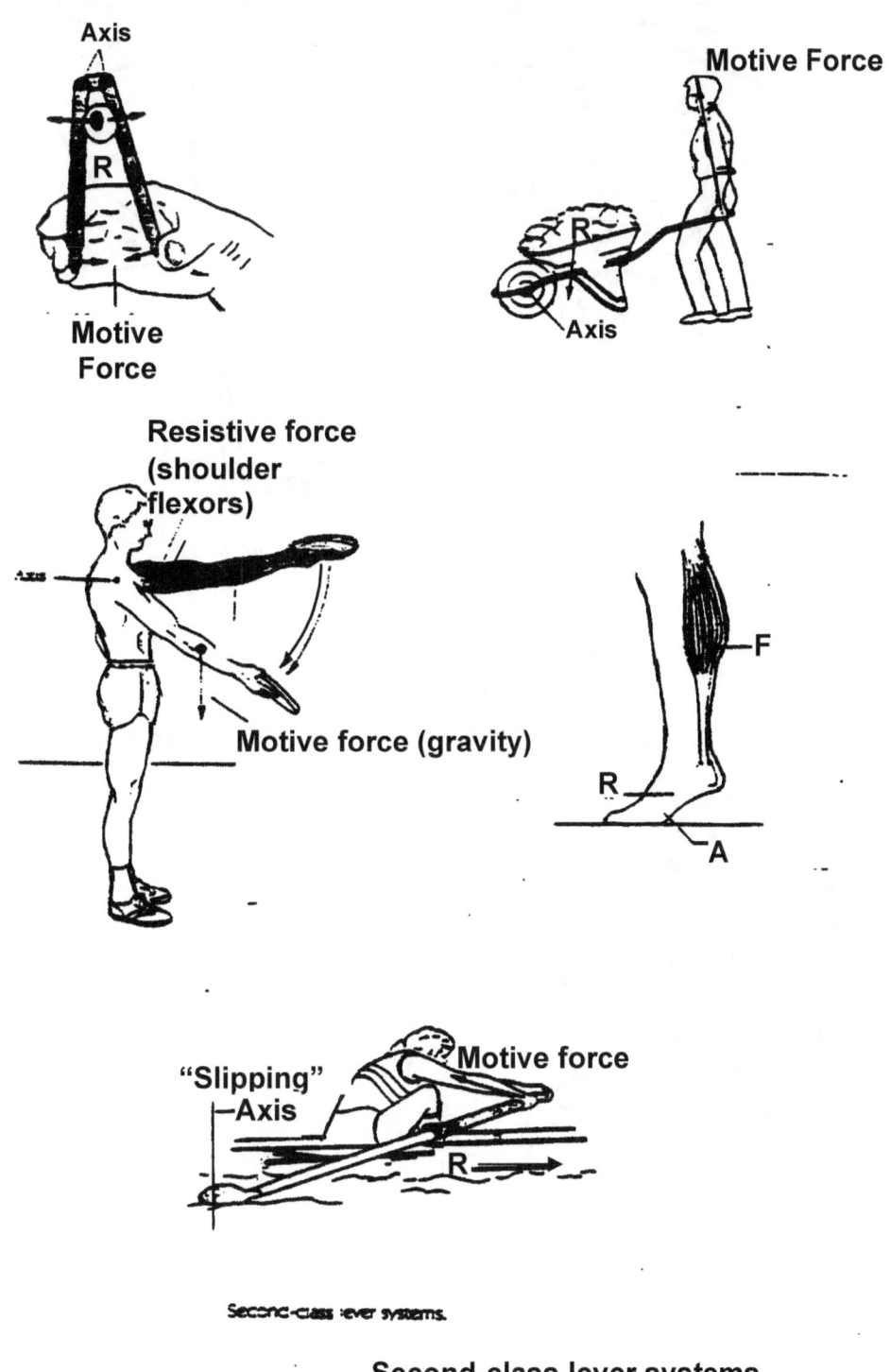

Second-class lever systems

Third-class lever - the force works at a point between the axis and the resistance (resistance arm is always longer than the force arm).

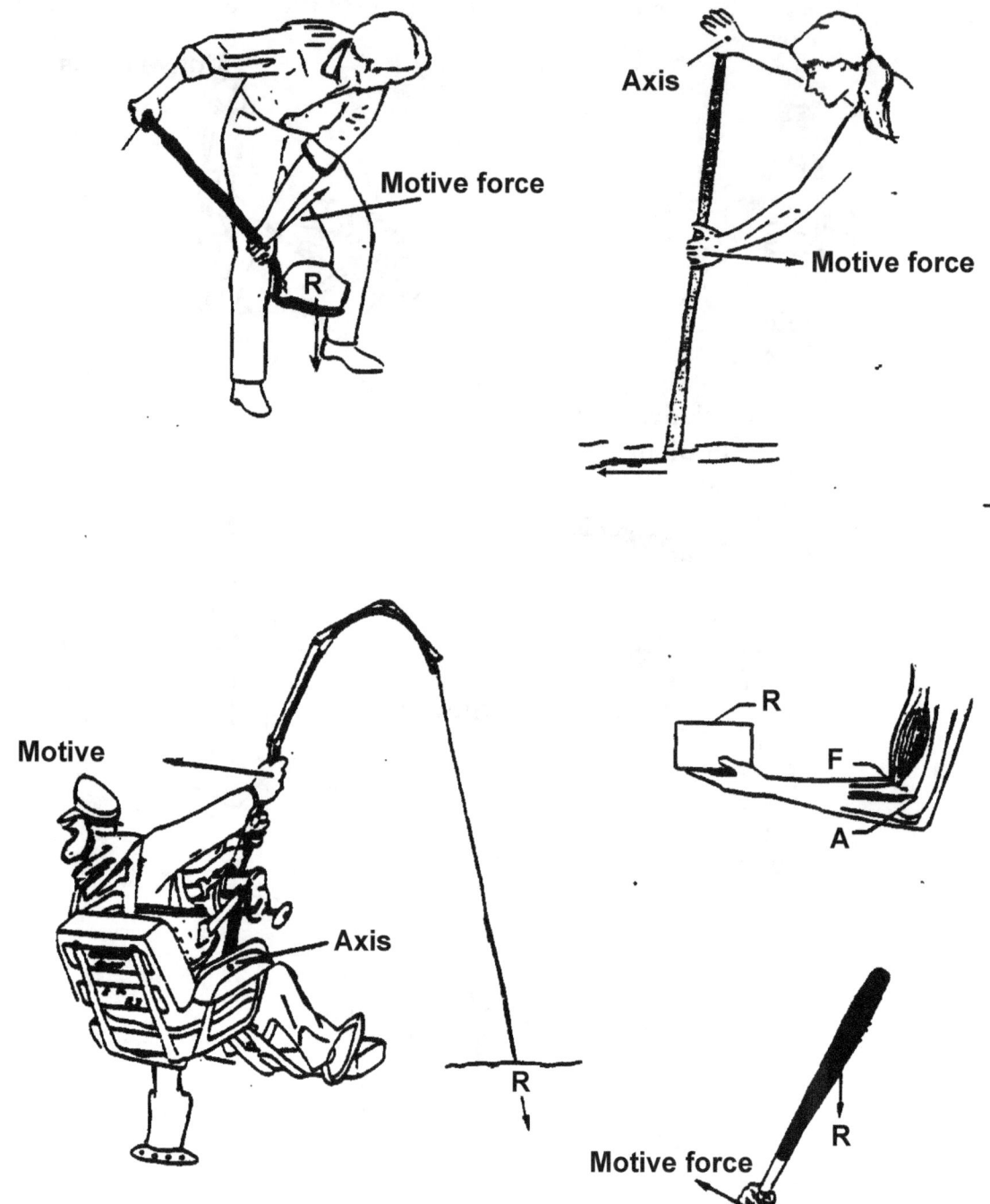

Muscle force is applied where muscles insert on bones.

With a few exceptions, the body consists primarily of third-class levers, with bones functioning as the levers and contracting innervated muscles acting as the fulcrums or by gravity acting on various body masses. As a result, the human body favors speed and range of motion over force.

Because most human body levers are long, their distal ends can move rapidly. Thus, the body is capable of swift, wide movements at the expense of abundant muscle force.

The human body easily performs tasks involving rapid movement with light objects. Very heavy tasks require a device for the body to secure an advantage of force.

Sports instruments increase body levers, thereby increasing the speed of an object's imparting force. However, the use of sports instruments requires more muscle force.

The body's leverage rarely includes one part of the body (a simple, singular lever). Movement of the body is an outcome of a system of levers operating together. However, levers do function in sequence when the force produced by the system of levers is dependent on the speed at the extremity. Many levers function simultaneously for a heavy task (e.g. pushing).

SKILL 5.3 Application of basic principles to sports skills

MECHANICAL PRINCIPLES OF MOTION APPLIED TO PHYSICAL EDUCATION ACTIVITIES

1. **Inertia** - tendency of a body or object to remain in its present state of motion; an object will stay in a prescribed straight path and will move at its given speed unless some force acts to change it.

2. **Projecting objects for vertical distance** - the forces of gravity and air resistance prevent vertically projected objects from continuing at their initial velocities. The downward, resistive force of gravity slows a projectile directed upward until it halts (at the peak of vertical path). At this point, the downward force of gravity becomes an incentive force that increases the speed of the object until it confronts another force (the earth or other external object) that slows the object until it stops. When the object stops ascending and begins to descend, gravity alters the object's direction of motion. Air resistance (of still air) always opposes the object's motion. Therefore, an ascending object's air resistance is downward and a descending object's air resistance is upward. An increase in velocity increases air-drag force that decreases the magnitude of the drag as the object moves upward, slowing in velocity. The magnitude of the drag increases as the object moves downwards faster and faster.

The direction and magnitude of the object's acceleration, due to the force of gravity, are constant. The direction and magnitude of changes due to air resistance are dependent on the object's speed and direction.

An object travels the highest when projected with the greatest velocity, and the object's weight affects neither gravity's upward deceleration nor its downward acceleration. The object's weight, however, is a factor in calculating the net force acting on the object's vertical movement through the air.

- **Projecting the body for vertical distance** - for these activities (e.g. vertical leaping), the height of reach of the hand from the ground is the significant factor. The following three factors determine the body's reach height: 1) the center of gravity's vertical velocity, 2) the center of gravity's height from the ground at takeoff, and 3) the vertical distance of the fingertips relative to the center of gravity at the peak of the jump.

- **Projecting for vertical distance with a horizontal component** - for these activities (e.g. high jumping), a running approach to the point of takeoff produces some horizontal velocity even with a 100% vertical takeoff.

- **Projecting for horizontal distance** - a body will continue to travel horizontally until an external force, usually the ground, halts it. Gravity stops vertical movement while ground friction eventually stops horizontal velocity, preventing any additional horizontal distance. "Air time" increases when the initial upward vertical velocity component is greater. There is a tradeoff between maximum "air time" (determined by vertical velocity) and maximum horizontal distance (determined by horizontal velocity).

- **Horizontal projections where takeoff and landing heights are equal** - maximum horizontal distance occurs when the projection angle is 45-degrees.

- **Horizontal projections where takeoff and landing heights are uneven** – the height of an object's center of gravity depends on a performer's height and his/her location in relation to the ground upon release or impact of the object. The greater the object's travel time forward, the farther the object's distance before landing. Hence, a taller performer has an automatic advantage over a shorter performer who throws with the same projection velocity. In addition, the greater the difference between takeoff and landing heights, the smaller the optimum angle of release - given equal projection velocities.

Projecting objects for accuracy:

- **Vertical plane targets** - accuracy is easiest when using a trajectory that is perpendicular to the target as it coincides with the target face. As projection distance increases, a more curved parabolic path is required.

- **Horizontal plane targets** - the more vertically the projectile arrives at the target (as close to 90 degrees as possible), the greater the likelihood of successfully hitting the target and preventing the object from rolling or sliding away from the target area.

Projecting the body for accuracy - for moving or positioning the body (or its segments) to achieve an ideal/model performance by body maneuvers, the performer projects his body's center of gravity to an imaginary target point in space.

Projecting objects for accuracy when speed may enhance the performance - the performer must increase the angle of projection for slower projection speeds (must consider participant's height).

- **Acceleration** - the movement response (acceleration) of a system depends not only on the net external force applied, but also depends on the resistance to movement change (inertia).

If an object's acceleration is proportional to the applied force, greater force produces greater acceleration. An object's acceleration is inversely proportional to its mass (the greater the mass, the lesser the acceleration).

- **Angular acceleration** (rate that an object's angular speed or direction changes) - angular acceleration is great when there is a large change in angular velocity in a short amount of time. A rigid body (or segment) encounters angular acceleration or deceleration only when a net external torque is applied. When torque stops, a new velocity is reached and maintained until another torque occurs. Acceleration is always in the direction of the acting torque, and the greater the torque, the greater the angular acceleration.

- **Linear acceleration** (time rate of change in velocity) - an object's magnitude of acceleration is significant if there is a large change of velocity in a small amount of time. When the same velocity changes over a longer period of time, acceleration is small. Acceleration occurs only when force is applied. When the force stops, the object/body reaches a new speed. The object/body continues at the new speed until a force changes the speed or direction. In addition, the direction of acceleration is same as the direction of the applied net force. A large force produces a large acceleration. A small force produces a modest acceleration.

- **Zero/Constant Acceleration** (constant velocity) - there is no change in a system's velocity when the object/body moves at a given velocity and encounters equal, opposing forces. Velocity is constant since no force causes acceleration or deceleration.

- **Acceleration caused by gravity** - a falling object/body continues to accelerate at the rate of 9.8 m/sec. (32 ft/sec.) throughout its fall.

- **Radial acceleration (direction change caused by centripetal force)** - centripetal force is aimed along an illusory line (the circular path) at any instant. Therefore, it is the force responsible for change of direction. The bigger the mass, the greater the centripetal force required. A tighter turn magnifies direction change (radial acceleration), so friction must increase to offset the increased acceleration. Maximum friction (centrifugal force) reduces speed. A combination of variables mass, radius of curvature, speed of travel, and centripetal force cause radial acceleration.

Action/Reaction - every action has an equal and opposite reaction.

- **Linear motion** - the larger the mass, the more it resists motion change initiated by an outside force.

Body segments exert forces against surfaces they contact. These forces and the reaction of the surfaces result in body movement. For example, a runner propels himself forward by exerting a force on the ground (as long as the surface has sufficient friction and resistance to slipping). The force of the contact of the runner's foot with the ground and the equal and opposite reaction of the ground produces movement. A canoe paddler or swimmer exerts a backward force by pushing the water backwards, causing a specific velocity that is dependent on the stroke's force. This along with the equal and opposite force made by the water pushing forward against the canoe paddle or arm moves the canoe or swimmer forward.

Every torque (angular motion) exerted by one body/object on another has another torque equal in magnitude and opposite in direction exerted by the second body/object on the first. Changing angular momentum requires a force that is equal and opposite of the change in momentum.

Performing actions in a standing position requires the counter pressure of the ground against the feet for accurate movement of one or more parts of the body.

KNOWLEDGE OF ACTIVITIES FOR BODY MANAGEMENT SKILL DEVELOPMENT

Sequential development and activities for locomotor skills acquisition

Sequential Development = crawl, creep, walk, run, jump, hop, gallop, slide, leap, skip, step-hop.

- **Activities to develop walking skills** include walking slower and faster in place; walking forward, backward, and sideways with slower and faster paces in straight, curving, and zigzag pathways with various lengths of steps; pausing between steps; and changing the height of the body.

- **Activities to develop running skills** include having students pretend they are playing basketball, trying to score a touchdown, trying to catch a bus, finishing a lengthy race, or running on a hot surface.

- **Activities to develop jumping skills** include alternating jumping with feet together and feet apart, taking off and landing on the balls of the feet, clicking the heels together while airborne, and landing with a foot forward and a foot backward.

- **Activities to develop galloping skills** include having students play a game of Fox and Hound, with the lead foot representing the fox and the back foot the hound trying to catch the fox (alternate the lead foot).

- **Activities to develop sliding skills** include having students hold hands in a circle and sliding in one direction, then sliding in the other direction.

- **Activities to develop hopping skills** include having students hop all the way around a hoop and hopping in and out of a hoop reversing direction. Students can also place ropes in straight lines and hop side-to-side over the rope from one end to the other and change (reverse) the direction.

- **Activities to develop skipping skills** include having students combine walking and hopping activities leading up to skipping.

- **Activities to develop step-hopping skills** include having students practice stepping and hopping activities while clapping hands to an uneven beat.

Sequential development and activities for nonlocomotor skill acquisition

Sequential Development = stretch, bend, sit, shake, turn, rock and sway, swing, twist, dodge, and fall.

- **Activities to develop stretching** include lying on the back and stomach and stretching as far as possible; stretching as though one is reaching for a star, picking fruit off a tree, climbing a ladder, shooting a basketball, or placing an item on a high self; waking and yawning.

- **Activities to develop bending** include touching knees and toes then straightening the entire body and straightening the body halfway; bending as though picking up a coin, tying shoes, picking flowers/vegetables, and petting animals of different sizes.

- **Activities to develop sitting** include practicing sitting from standing, kneeling, and lying positions without the use of hands.

- **Activities to develop falling skills** include first collapsing in one's own space and then pretending to fall like bowling pins, raindrops, snowflakes, a rag doll, or Humpty Dumpty.

Sequential development and activities for manipulative skill development

Sequential Development = striking, throwing, kicking, ball rolling, volleying, bouncing, catching, and trapping.

- **Activities to develop striking** begin with the striking of stationary objects by a participant in a stationary position. Next, the person remains still while trying to strike a moving object. Then, both the object and the participant are in motion as the participant attempts to strike the moving object.

- **Activities to develop throwing** include throwing yarn/foam balls against a wall, then at a big target, and finally at targets decreasing in size.

- **Activities to develop kicking** include alternating feet to kick balloons/beach balls, then kicking them under and over ropes. Change the type of ball as proficiency develops.

- **Activities to develop ball rolling** include rolling different sized balls to a wall, then to targets decreasing in size.

- **Activities to develop volleying** include using a large balloon and, first, hitting it with both hands, then one hand (alternating hands), and then using different parts of the body. Change the object as students progress (balloon, to beach ball, to foam ball, etc.)

- **Activities to develop bouncing** include starting with large balls and, first, using both hands to bounce and then using one hand (alternate hands).

- **Activities to develop catching** include using various objects (balloons, beanbags, balls, etc.) to catch. First, catch the object the participant has thrown himself/herself, then catch objects someone else has thrown, and finally increase the distance between the catcher and the thrower.

- **Activities to develop trapping** include trapping slow and fast rolling balls; trapping balls (or other objects such as beanbags) that are lightly thrown at waist, chest, and stomach levels; trapping different size balls.

SKILL 5.4 Methods for analyzing movement

ANALYSIS OF MOTOR PERFORMANCE

Errors in skill performance

Because performing a skill has several components, determining why a participant is performing poorly may be difficult. Instructors may have to assess several components of a skill to determine the root cause of poor performance and appropriately correct errors. **An instructor should have the ability to identify performance errors by observing a student's mechanical principles of motion during the performance of a skill. Process assessment** is a subjective, observational approach to identifying errors in the form, style, or mechanics of a skill.

Appropriate objective measurements of fundamental skills

Instructors should use **product assessments**, quantitative measures of a movement's end result, to evaluate objectively fundamental skills. How far, fast, or high; or how many are the quantitative measures of product assessments.

A **criterion-referenced test** (superior to a standardized test) or a **standardized norm-referenced test** can provide valid and reliable data for objectively measuring fundamental skills.

Use skill assessment information to plan error correction strategies

Instructors can use criterion-referenced standards to diagnose weaknesses and correct errors in skill performance because such performance standards define appropriate levels of achievement. However, instructors can also use biomechanical instructional objectives. The following list describes the skill assessment criteria in several representative activities:

- Archery - measuring accuracy in shooting a standardized target from a specified place.

- Bowling - calculating the bowling average attained under standardized conditions.

- Golf - the score after several rounds.

- Swimming - counting the number of breaststrokes needed to swim 25 yards.

After assessing student skill performance, the instructor should design drills or tasks that will develop the weakest component of the student's performance. For example, an instructor notices that a group of students attempting to shoot basketball free throw shots cannot get the ball to the basket because they do not use their legs to add power to the shot. The instructor should use this observation to construct drills that encourage leg use and develop strength.

SKILL 5.5 Analysis of basic movement patters: overhand throw, underhand throw, kick

OVERHAND THROW

The overhand throw consists of a sequence of four movements: a stride, hip rotation, trunk rotation, and forward arm movement. The thrower should align his body sideways to the target (with opposite shoulder pointing towards the target). The overhand throw begins with a step or stride with the opposite foot (i.e. left foot for a right-handed thrower). As the stride foot contacts the ground, the pivot foot braces against the ground and provides stability for the subsequent movements. Hip rotation is the natural turning of the hips toward the target. Trunk rotation follows hip rotation. The hips should rotate before the trunk because the stretching of the torso muscles allows for stronger muscle contraction during trunk rotation. Following trunk rotation, the arm moves forward in two phases. In the first phase the elbow is bent. In the second phase, the elbow joint straightens and the thrower releases the ball.

Development of the overhand throwing motion in children occurs in three stages: elementary, mature, and advanced. In the elementary stage, the child throws mainly with the arm and does not incorporate other body movements. The signature characteristic of this stage is striding with the foot on the same side of the body as the throwing arm (i.e. placing the right foot in front when throwing with the right hand). In the mature stage, the thrower brings the arm backward in preparation for the throw. Use of body rotation is still limited. Children in the advanced stage incorporate all the elements of the overhand throw. The thrower displays an obvious stride and body rotation.

UNDERHAND THROW

The thrower places the object in the dominant hand. When drawing the arm back the triceps straighten the elbow and, depending on the amount of power behind the throw, the shoulder extends or hyper extends using the posterior deltoid, latissimus dorsi, and the teres major. At the time of drawback, a step forward is taken with the leg opposite to the throwing arm. When coming back down, the thrower moves the shoulder muscles (primarily the anterior deltoid) into flexion. When the object in hand moves in front of the body, the thrower releases the ball. The wrist may be firm or slightly flexed. The thrower releases the object shortly after planting the foot and the biceps muscle contracts, moving the elbow into flexion during follow through.

KICK

In executing a kick, the object needs to be in front of the body and in front of the dominant leg. The kicker steps and plants with the opposite leg while drawing the kicking leg back. During draw back, the hamstring muscle group flexes the knee. When the kicker plants the opposite foot, the hips swing forward for power and the knee moves into extension using the quadriceps muscle group. The contact point is approximately even with the plant foot and a comfortable follow through completes the action.

COMPETENCY 6.0   HEALTH AND SAFETY

SKILL 6.1   Safety and injury prevention: general and specific safety considerations for all movement activities; fitness-related safety considerations, such as warm-up/cool-down, harmful exercise techniques, and environmental conditions

ACTIONS THAT PROMOTE SAFETY AND INJURY PREVENTION

1. Having an instructor who is properly trained and qualified.

2. Organizing the class by size, activity, and conditions of the class.

3. Inspecting buildings and other facilities regularly and immediately giving notice of any hazards.

4. Avoiding overcrowding.

5. Using adequate lighting.

6. Ensuring that students dress in appropriate clothing and shoes.

7. Presenting organized activities.

8. Inspecting all equipment regularly.

9. Adhering to building codes and fire regulations.

10. Using protective equipment.

11. Using spotters.

12. Eliminating hazards.

13. Teaching students correct ways to perform skills and activities.

14. Teaching students how to use the equipment properly and safely.

GENERAL AND SPECIFIC SAFETY CONSIDERATIONS FOR ALL MOVEMENT ACTIVITIES

Aquatics

To promote **water safety**, physical education instructors should make students familiar with appropriate medical responses to life-threatening situations (e.g. recognizing signs that someone needs medical attention – not moving, not breathing, etc.; knowledge of the proper response – who to contact and where to find them). With older children, instructors can introduce rudimentary first aid training. Finally, instructors must ensure that students are aware and observant of safety rules (e.g. no running near the water, no chewing gum while swimming, no swimming without a lifeguard, no roughhousing near or in the water, etc.).

Outdoor education

Related safety education should emphasize the importance of planning and research. Instructors should ask students to consider in advance what the potential dangers of an activity might be, and to prepare and plan accordingly. Of course, educator supervision is required. Outdoor education activities require first-aid equipment and properly trained educators. Students should use appropriate safety gear (e.g. helmets, harnesses, etc.). Instructors should generally obtain parental consent for outdoor education activities.

Combative activities

Related safety issues include stressing the potential harm that these activities can cause (stressing specific damage potential to musculoskeletal systems), emphasizing students' responsibility for the well-being of their training partners, maintaining discipline throughout the class (ensuring students remain focused on their training activities and alert to the instructor's instructions), and ensuring that students are aware and observant of the limits to force that they may apply (e.g. no-striking zones, like above the neck and below the belt; limits on striking force, like semi-contact or no-contact sparring; familiarity with the concept of a tap-out indicating submission). Students should perform warm-up, cool-down, and stretching as with any physical training program.

TECHNIQUES AND BENEFITS OF WARMING UP AND COOLING DOWN

Warming up is a gradual 5 to 10 minute aerobic warm-up in which the participant uses the muscles needed in the activity to follow (similar movements at a lower activity). Warm-ups also include stretching of major muscle groups after the gradual warm-up.

The benefits of warming up are:

- preparing the body for physical activity
- reducing the risk of musculoskeletal injuries
- releasing oxygen from myoglobin
- warming the body's inner core
- increasing the reaction of muscles
- bringing the heart rate to an aerobic conditioning level

Cooling down is similar to warming up - a moderate to light tapering-off of vigorous activity at the end of an exercise session.

The benefits of cooling down are:

- redistributing circulation of the blood throughout the body to prevent pooling of blood
- preventing dizziness
- facilitating the removal of lactic acid

IDENTIFYING EXERCISE EQUIPMENT AS EITHER SOUND OR UNSOUND USING PHYSIOLOGICAL PRINCIPLES

Rolling machines, vibrating belts, vibrating tables and pillows, massaging devices, electrical muscle stimulators, weighted belts, motor-driven cycles and rowing machines, saunas, and plastic or rubberized sweat and sauna suits **are all ineffective exercise equipment because they produce passive movement** (no voluntary muscle contractions).

Sound exercise equipment produces active movement resulting from the participant initiating the movement of the equipment or the participant voluntarily producing muscle contractions.

The more you analyze exercise equipment available in the market the more you may wonder who is actually creating it. For example, equipment that has weight increments measured as light, medium, or difficult, is unsound. Such ambiguous labeling depends on who is using the equipment and their level of proficiency.

Some equipment is said to use all muscle groups at once. Just three minutes a day is as good as a total gym workout. Such claims are certainly false.

But what is good equipment? Good equipment uses a safe range of motion, safe increments of weight progression, and is structurally sound. The components of good equipment are reliable and not likely to cause injury. Safe equipment can consist of a combination of pieces that, when used correctly, improve physiological processes by guiding range of motion.

PHYSICAL EDUCATION SUPERVISION AND MANAGEMENT

Strategies for injury prevention

Participant screenings – evaluate injury history, anticipate and prevent potential injuries, watch for hidden injuries and reoccurrence of an injury, and maintain communication.

Standards and discipline – ensure that athletes obey rules of sportsmanship, supervision, and biomechanics.

Education and knowledge – stay current with the knowledge of first aid, sports medicine, sport technique, and injury prevention through clinics, workshops, and communication with staff and trainers.

Conditioning – programs should be year long and participants should have access to conditioning facilities in and out of season. This will produce more fit and knowledgeable athletes that are less prone to injury.

Equipment – perform regular inspections; ensure proper fit and proper use.

Facilities – maintain standards and use safe equipment.

Field care – establish emergency procedures for serious injury.

Rehabilitation – use objective measures such as power output on an isokinetic dynamometer.

Prevention of common athletic injuries

Foot – start with good footwear, foot exercises.

Ankle – use high top shoes and tape support; strengthen plantar (calf), dorsiflexor (shin), and ankle eversion (ankle outward).

Shin splints – strengthen ankle dorsiflexors.

Achilles tendon – stretch dorsiflexion and strengthen plantar flexion (heel raises).

Knee – increase strength and flexibility of calf and thigh muscles.

Back – use proper body mechanics.

Tennis elbow – lateral epicondylitis caused by bent elbow, hitting late, not stepping into the ball, heavy rackets, and rackets that are strung too tight.

Head and neck injuries – avoid dangerous techniques (i.e. grabbing face mask) and carefully supervise dangerous activities like the trampoline.

School officials and instructors should base **equipment selection** on quality and safety; goals of physical education and athletics; participants interests, age, sex, skills, and limitations; and trends in athletic equipment and uniforms. Knowledgeable personnel should select the equipment keeping in mind continuous service and replacement considerations (i.e. what's best in year of selection may not be best the following year). One final consideration is the possibility of reconditioning versus the purchase of new equipment.

HARMFUL EXERCISE TECHNIQUES AND ENVIRONMENTAL CONDITIONS

Instructors and participants should make safety and injury prevention top priority in exercise activities. There are a number of potential risks associated with physical activity, and instructors must be familiar with all the risks to prevent an emergency situation.

Equipment

Exercise equipment in poor condition has the potential for malfunction. Instructors should perform weekly checks to ensure all equipment is in proper working order. If it is not, the instructor or maintenance staff must repair the equipment before students use it. Placement of exercise equipment is also important. There should be adequate space between machines and benches to ensure a safe environment.

Technique

Instructors should stress proper exercise technique at all times, especially with beginners to prevent development of bad habits. Whether it's weightlifting, running, or stretching, participants should not force any body part beyond the normal range of motion. Pain is a good indicator of overextension. Living by the phrase, "No pain, no gain", is potentially dangerous. Participants should use slow and controlled movements. In addition, participants must engage in proper warm-up and cool-down before and after exercise. When lifting weights, lifters should always have a partner. A spotter can help correct the lifter's technique and help lift the weight to safety if the lifter is unable to do so. A partner can also offer encouragement and motivation. Flexibility is an often overlooked, yet important, part of exercise that can play a key role in injury prevention. Participants should perform stretching exercises after each workout session.

Environment

Environmental conditions can be very dangerous and potentially life threatening. Be cautious when exercising in extremely hot, cold, and/or humid conditions. High humidity can slow the body's release of heat from the body, increasing the chances of heat related illnesses. Hydration in hot environments is very important. Drink two cups of water two hours before exercise and hydrate regularly during exercise at the same rate at which the sweat is lost. While performing exercise lasting a long period of time, it is possible to drink too much water, resulting in a condition known as hyponutremia, or low sodium content in the body. Water cannot replace sodium and other electrolytes lost through sweat. Drinking sports drinks can solve this problem. Cold environments can also be a problem when exercising. The human body works more efficiently at its normal temperature. Wear many layers of clothing to prevent cold-related illnesses such as frostbite and hypothermia. In populations suffering from asthma, wearing a cloth over the mouth during exercise increases the moisture of the air breathed in and can help prevent an attack.

EQUIPMENT AND FACILITY SELECTION AND MAINTENANCE

Additional Guidelines for Selection of Equipment

- follow purchasing policies
- relate purchasing to program, budget, and finances
- consider maintenance
- abide by legal regulations
- recognize administrative considerations (good working relationships at all personnel levels)
- determine best value for money spent
- ensure that participants have own equipment and supplies when necessary
- purchase from reputable manufacturers and distributors
- follow competitive purchasing regulations
- use school forms with clearly identified brand, trademark, and catalog specifications

Equipment Maintenance Procedures

- inspect supplies and equipment upon arrival
- label supplies and equipment with organization's identification
- have policies for issuing and returning supplies and equipment
- keep equipment in perfect operating condition
- store properly
- properly clean and care for equipment (including garments)

Facility Selection Considerations

- bond issues for construction
- availability to girls, women, minorities, and the handicapped
- energy costs and conservation
- community involvement
- convertibility (movable walls/partitions)
- environment must be safe, attractive, clean, comfortable, practical, and adaptable to individual needs
- compliance with public health codes
- effective disease control

Facility Maintenance Procedures

- custodial staff, participants, and the physical education and athletic staffs must work together to properly maintain facility
- Pools need daily monitoring of water temperature, hydrogen ion concentration, and chlorine
- gymnasium play areas must be free from dust and dirt
- showers and drying areas need daily cleaning and disinfecting
- participants' clothing should meet health standards to prevent odor and bacterial growth

- outdoor playing fields must be clear of rocks and free of holes and uneven surfaces

- disinfect and clean drinking fountains, sinks, urinals, and toilets daily

- air out and sanitize lockers frequently.

SKILL 6.2 **Health appraisals and referrals: health-related fitness appraisals; personal goal-setting and assessment, such as Physical Best, President's Challenge, and Fitnessgram; considerations related to the Individuals with Disabilities Education Act**

FITNESS APPRAISALS

The trend in physical education assessment is to move increasingly away from norm- and criterion-referenced evaluations (i.e. measuring a student's achievements against the achievements of a normative group or against criteria that are arbitrarily set by either the educator or the governing educational body), and towards performance-based, or "authentic" evaluations. This creates difficulty for physical educators because it eliminates preset reference points.

The advantage of performance-based evaluations is they are equally fair to individuals with diverse backgrounds, special needs, and disabilities. In all cases, the instructor evaluates students based on their personal performance.

Portfolio construction is one way of assessing the performance of a student. The student chooses the achievements to add to the portfolio. This creates a tool that assesses current abilities and serves as a benchmark against which the instructor can measure future performance (thus evaluating progress over time, and not just a localized achievement).

Student self-assessment is often an important part of portfolios. The instructor should ask children questions like, "Where am I now? Where am I trying to go? What am I trying to achieve? How can I get from here to there?" This type of questioning involves the child more deeply in the learning process.

TYPES OF EVALUATION

Summative evaluation strategies involve assigning the student a letter or number grade, which can reflect both the student's performance and progress. Examples include:

- Performance evaluations – the instructor assigns a letter or number grade based on the student's performance on a task or set of tasks (e.g. push-ups and sit-ups, time to run one mile, etc.).

- Progress evaluations – the instructor assigns a letter or number grade based on the student's improvement in the ability to perform a task or set of tasks.

- Effort evaluations – the instructor assigns a letter or number grade based on the student's effort in working towards training goals.

- Behavior evaluations – the instructor assigns a letter or number grade based on the student's behavior in and attitude towards training and the training environment.

Formative evaluation strategies do not provide a letter or number grade to the student. It focuses on a textual analysis of the student's performance and progress. Examples include a written analysis of the student's performance, progress, effort, attitude, and behavior.

SPECIFIC PHYSICAL FITNESS APPRAISALS

The following is a list of tests that instructors can use to assess the physical fitness of students.

Cardio-respiratory fitness tests – maximal stress test, sub maximal stress test, Bruce Protocol, Balke Protocol, Astrand and Rhyming Test, PWC Test, Bench Step Test, Rockport Walking Fitness Test, and Cooper 1.5 Mile Run/Walk Fitness Test.

Muscle strength tests – dynamometers (hand, back, and leg), cable tensiometer, The 1-RM Test (repetition maximum: bench press, standing press, arm curl, and leg press), bench-squat, sit-ups (one sit up holding a weight plate behind the neck), and lateral pull-down.

Muscle endurance tests – squat-thrust, pull-ups, sit-ups, lateral pull-down, bench-press, arm curl, push-ups, and dips.

Flexibility tests – sit and reach, Kraus-Webber Floor Touch Test, trunk extension, forward bend of trunk, Leighton Flexometer, shoulder rotation/flexion, and goniometer.

Body Composition determination – Hydrostatic weighing, skin fold measurements, limb/girth circumference, and body mass index.

Agility tests – Illinois Agility Run.

Balance tests – Bass Test of Dynamic Balance (lengthwise and crosswise), Johnson Modification of the Bass Test of Dynamic Balance, modified sideward leap, and balance beam walk.

Coordination tests – Stick test of Coordination.

Power tests – vertical jump.

Speed tests – 50-yard dash.

GOAL-SETTING AND ASSESSMENT

Goal setting is an effective way of achieving progress. In order to preserve and/or increase self-confidence, you and your students must set goals that are frequently reachable. One such way of achieving this is to set several small, short-term goals to attain one long-term goal. Be realistic in goal setting to increase fitness levels gradually. As students reach their goals, set more in order to continue performance improvement. Keep in mind that maintaining a current fitness level is an adequate goal provided the individual is in a healthy state. Reward your students when they reach goals. Rewards serve as motivation to reach the next goal. Also, be sure to prepare for lapses. Try to get back on track as soon as possible.

To help realize fitness goals, several organizations exist to educate and encourage physical fitness. Three such programs include Physical Best, President's Challenge, and Fitnessgram.

Physical Best is a comprehensive health-related fitness education program developed by physical educators for physical educators. The purpose of Physical Best is to educate, challenge, and encourage all children to develop the knowledge, skills, and attitudes for a healthy and fit life. The goal of the program is to move students from dependence to independence for their own fitness and health by promoting regular, enjoyable physical activity. The focus of Physical Best is to educate ALL children regardless of athletic talent, physical, and mental abilities or disabilities. http://www.aahperd.org/NASPE/physicalbest/

The President's Challenge is a program that encourages all Americans to make regular physical activity a part of their everyday lives. No matter what your activity and fitness level, the President's Challenge can help motivate you to improve. http://www.presidentschallenge.org/

The Cooper Institute in Dallas, Texas introduced Fitnessgram in 1982. The objective was to increase parental awareness of children's fitness levels. This was done by developing an easy way for physical education teachers to report the results of physical fitness assessments.
http://www.cooperinst.org/ftginfo.asp#Overview

HUMAN DEVELOPMENT, MOTOR BEHAVIOR, AND PRESCRIBED EXERCISES

Instructors must consider student disabilities and specific needs when setting personal fitness goals. Instructors should evaluate proposed activities and set standards for desired motor behavioral change taking into account the diverse student population.

Standards for measures of success and evaluation include parameters that set the bench marks for change in motor related skills and stock knowledge. A special criterion is set for students with disabilities and special needs in consonance with the Individuals with Disabilities Education Act (IDEA).

SKILL 6.3 Handling accidents and illnesses: first aid, CPR, water safety, certification

EMERGENCY ACTION PLANS

The first step in establishing a safe physical education environment is creating an Emergency Action Plan (EAP). The formation of a well-planned EAP can make a significant difference in the outcome of an injury situation. Each district requires a school-wide consistent Emergency Action Plan that is to be followed. Physical education teachers need to know this plan and review it often.

Components of an Emergency Action Plan
To ensure the safety of students during physical activity, an EAP should be easily comprehensible yet detailed enough to facilitate prompt, thorough action.

Communication
Instructors should communicate rules and expectations clearly to students. This information should include pre-participation guidelines, emergency procedures, and proper game etiquette. Instructors should collect emergency information sheets from students at the start of each school year. First-aid kits, facility maps, and incident report forms should also be readily available. Open communication between students and teachers is essential. Creating a positive environment within the classroom allows students to feel comfortable enough to approach an adult/teacher if she feels she has sustained a potential injury.

Teacher Education
At the start of each school year, every student should undergo a pre-participation physical examination. This allows a teacher to recognize the "high-risk" students before activity commences. The teacher should also take note of any student that requires any form of medication or special care. When a teacher is aware of his/her students' conditions, the learning environment is a lot safer.

Facilities and Equipment
It is the responsibility of the teacher and school district to provide a safe environment, playing area, and equipment for students. Instructors and maintenance staff should regularly inspect school facilities to confirm that the equipment and location is adequate and safe for student use.

First Aid Equipment
It is essential to have a properly stocked first aid kit in an easily reachable location. Instructors may need to include asthma inhalers and special care items to meet the specific needs of certain students. Instructors should clearly mark these special care items to avoid a potential harmful mix-up.

Implementing the Emergency Plan
The main thing to keep in mind when implementing an EAP is to remain calm. Maintaining a sufficient level of control and activating appropriate medical assistance will facilitate the process and will leave less room for error.

STRATEGIES FOR INJURY PREVENTION

Participant screenings – evaluate injury history, anticipate and prevent potential injuries, watch for hidden injuries and reoccurrence of an injury, and maintain communication.

Standards and discipline – ensure that athletes obey rules of sportsmanship, supervision, and biomechanics.

Education and knowledge – stay current with knowledge of first aid, sports medicine, sport technique, and injury prevention through clinics, workshops, and communication with staff and trainers.

Conditioning – programs should be year long and participants should have access to conditioning facilities in and out of season. This will produce more fit and knowledgeable athletes who are less prone to injury.

Equipment – perform regular inspections; ensure proper fit and proper use.

Facilities – maintain standards and use safe equipment.

Field care – establish emergency procedures for serious injury.

Rehabilitation – use objective measures such as power output on an isokinetic dynamometer.

Weather Conditions- use common sense and always err on the side of caution in extreme heat/cold or possible stormy weather conditions

PREVENTION OF COMMON ATHLETIC INJURIES

Foot – start with good footwear, foot exercises.

Ankle – use high top shoes and tape support; strengthen plantar (calf), dorsiflexor (shin), and ankle eversion (ankle outward).

Shin splints – strengthen ankle dorsiflexors.

Achilles tendon – stretch dorsiflexion and strengthen plantar flexion (heel raises).

Knee – increase strength and flexibility of calf and thigh muscles.

Back – use proper body mechanics.

Tennis elbow – lateral epicondylitis caused by bent elbow, hitting late, not stepping into the ball, heavy rackets, and rackets that are strung too tight.

Head and neck injuries – avoid dangerous techniques (i.e. grabbing face mask) and carefully supervise dangerous activities like the trampoline.

CARE FOR COMMON ATHLETIC INJURIES

The most common injuries that physical education instructors will encounter include muscle sprains and strains, soft tissue injuries, and cuts and bruises. Instructors should apply the RICE principle when caring for muscle sprains, strains, and soft tissue injuries. The RICE principle stands for: rest, ice, compression, and elevation.

- **Rest** – injured students should stop using the injured body part immediately
- **Ice** – the instructor should apply ice to the injured area to help reduce swelling
- **Compression** – the instructor should wrap the injured area to help reduce swelling
- **Elevation** – the student should raise the injured area above heart level

In addition, physical education instructors should have a well-stocked first aid kit that allows the treatment of routine cuts and bruises. Finally, instructors must recognize more serious injuries that require immediate medical attention. For example, injuries to the head or neck require medical attention and extreme caution.

Treating specific illnesses

Diabetes

Most children with diabetes suffer from Type 1 (insulin-dependent or juvenile) diabetes. Type 1 diabetes limits the pancreas' ability to produce insulin, a hormone vital to life. Without insulin, the body cannot use the sugar found in blood. In order to stay alive, an individual suffering from Type 1 diabetes must take one or more injections of insulin daily.

Diabetics control their disease by keeping the level of blood sugar (glucose) as close to normal as possible. The means to achieve diabetes control include proper nutrition, exercise, and insulin. Most children with diabetes self-monitor blood glucose levels to track their condition and respond to changes.

Some rules of thumb to keep in mind when dealing with a diabetic child are:

- Food makes the glucose level rise
- Exercise and insulin make the glucose level fall
- Hypoglycemia occurs when the blood sugar level is low
- Hyperglycemia occurs when the blood sugar level is high

Low Blood Sugar (Hypoglycemia)

This is the diabetic emergency most likely to occur. Low blood sugar may result from eating too little, engaging in too much physical activity without eating, or by injecting too much insulin.

Symptoms:
- Headache
- Sweating
- Shakiness
- Pale, moist skin
- Fatigue/Weakness
- Loss of coordination

Treatment:
Provide sugar immediately. You may give the student ½ cup of fruit juice, non-diet soda, or two to four glucose tablets. The child should feel better within the next 10 minutes. If so, the child should eat some additional food (e.g. half a peanut butter, meat, or cheese sandwich). If the child's status does not improve, treat the reaction again.

High Blood Sugar (Hyperglycemia)

Hyperglycemia can result from eating too much, engaging in too little physical activity, not injecting enough insulin, or illness. You can confirm high blood sugar levels by testing with a glucose meter.

Symptoms:
- Increased thirst
- Weakness/Fatigue
- Blurred vision
- Frequent urination
- Loss of appetite

Treatment:
If hyperglycemia occurs, the instructor should contact the student's parent or guardian immediately.

Dehydration
Dehydration occurs when a person loses more fluids than he/she takes in. The amount of water present in the body subsequently drops below the level needed for normal body functions. The two main causes of dehydration are gastrointestinal illness (vomiting, diarrhea) and sports. It is essential to replace fluids lost by sweating to prevent dehydration, especially on a hot day.

Symptoms:
- Thirst
- Dizziness
- Dry mouth
- Producing less/darker urine

Prevention/Treatment:
- Drink lots of fluids. Water is usually the best choice.
- Dress appropriately (i.e., loose-fitting clothes and a hat).
- If you begin to feel thirsty or dizzy, take a break and sit in the shade.
- Drink fluids prior to physical activity and then at 20 minute intervals after activity commences.
- Play sports or train in the early morning or late afternoon. You will avoid the hottest part of the day.

CPR BASICS

Cardiopulmonary resuscitation (CPR) is a first-aid technique used to keep cardiac arrest victims alive. It also prevents brain damage while the individual is unconscious and more advanced medical help is on the way. CPR keeps blood flowing through the body and in and out of the lungs.

CPR Steps
- Step 1 – Call 911
- Step 2 – Tilt head, lift chin, check breathing
- Step 3 – Give two breaths
- Step 4 – Position hands in the center of chest
- Step 5 – Firmly push down two inches on the chest 15 times

Continue with two breaths and 15 pumps until help arrives. The American Heart Association and the American Red Cross both offer classes to train individuals in CPR.

WATER SAFETY BASICS
- Get a partner. Even experienced swimmers get tired or get muscle cramps. When swimming with a partner you can help each other or go for help in case of an emergency.
- Learn some life-saving techniques (e.g. CPR).
- Know your limits. If you're a novice swimmer, don't go into water that is so deep that you're unable to touch the bottom. Also, don't try to keep up with advanced swimmers.
- Swim only in places with lifeguard supervision.
- When swimming in an open body of water, don't fight the current, swim with it, gradually trying to make your way to shore.
- Dive only in areas that are safe for diving.
- Watch the sun and reapply sunscreen often.
- Drink plenty of fluids to prevent dehydration from the sun.
- Don't stay in cool water for too long. This can lower your body temperature. Get out of the water if you feel your muscles cramp or you begin to shiver.
- Never mix alcohol and swimming.

SKILL 6.4 Knowledge of legal aspects in teaching physical education

ESTABLISHMENT OF CURRICULUM FRAMEWORKS AND STUDENT PERFORMANCE STANDARDS

A curriculum framework is a set of broad guidelines that aids educational personnel in producing specific instructional plans for a given subject or study area. The legislative intent was to promote a degree of **uniformity and instructional consistency** in curriculum offerings.

Student achievement is related to the intended outcomes of the selected curriculum frameworks. The legislature developed student performance standards for 40 physical education courses and 15 dance courses.

FEDERAL LEGISLATION

The Department of Health and Human Services recommended legislative changes - including those for education. **Title IX** prohibits sex discrimination in educational programs and **PL 94-142** requires schools to provide educational services for handicapped students.

STATE LEGISLATION

State governments (Department of Education) are primarily responsible for education. Departments of education establish policies for course curriculum, number of class days and class time, and amount of credits required for graduation.

IMPACT OF EDUCATION REFORMS

Enrollment went up and there was renewed administrative, parental, and student support. Additional impacts include: coeducational classes, separate teams for boys and girls and men and women (otherwise the school must create a coeducational team), equal opportunities for both sexes (for facilities, equipment and supplies, practice and games, medical and training services, academic tutoring and coaching, travel and per diem allowances, and dining and housing facilities), and equitable expenditure of funds for both sexes.

Title IX takes precedence over all conflicting state and local laws and conference regulations. Federal aid (even aid not related to physical education or athletics) must comply with Title IX. Finally, Title IX prohibits discrimination in personnel standards and scholarships selection.

LIABILITY CONCERNS IN PHYSICAL EDUCATION

Historically, common-law rules stated that individuals could not sue government agencies without consent of the agencies. However, federal and state courts have begun to allow individuals to sue both federal and state governments. Thus, public schools and school districts are now subject to liability lawsuits.

Compulsory elements of the school curriculum, such as physical education, prompt courts to decide based on what is in the best interests of the public.

Although school districts still have immunity in many states, teachers do not have such immunity. Whether employed by private person or a municipal corporation every employee owes a duty not to injure another by a negligent act of commission.

The following is a list of common legal terms and conditions applicable to physical education.

1. Tort – a legal wrong resulting in a direct or indirect injury; includes omissions and acts intended or unintended to cause harm.

2. Negligence – failing to fulfill a legal duty according to common reasoning; includes instruction and facility maintenance; instructors must consider sex, size, and skill of participants when planning activities and grouping students.

3. In Loco Parentis – acting in the place of the parent in relation to a child.

4. Sports Product Liability – liability of the manufacturer to the person using the manufacturer's product who sustains injury/damage from using the product.

5. Violence and legal liability (intentional injury in sports contests) – harmful, illegal contact of one person by another (referred to as battery).

6. Physical education classes held off campus and legal liability – primary concern is providing due care, which is the responsibility of management and staff members of sponsoring organization; failing to observe "due care" can result in findings of negligence.

7. Attractive Nuisance – an object that results in physical injury that the responsible party should have foreseen.

ACTIONS THAT CAN AVOID LAWSUITS

1. Knowing the health status of each person in the program.

2. Considering the ability and skill level of participants when planning new activities.

3. Grouping students to equalize competitive levels.

4. Using safe equipment and facilities.

5. Properly organizing and supervising classes.

6. Never leaving a class.

7. Knowing first aid (Do not diagnose or prescribe).

8. Keeping accident records.

9. Giving instruction prior to dangerous activities.

10. Being sure that injured students get medical attention and examination.

11. Getting exculpatory agreements (parental consent forms).

12. Having a planned, written disposition for students who suffer injuries or become ill.

13. Providing a detailed accident report if one occurs.

14. Join your local school district union. Unions provide liability insurance and legal representation, should the need arise.

SKILL 6.5 Effects of substance abuse on performance and behavior

Substance abuse can lead to adverse behaviors and increased risk of injury and disease. Any substance affecting the normal functions of the body, illegal or not, is potentially dangerous and students and athletes should avoid them completely.

Anabolic steroids – The alleged benefit is an increase in muscle mass and strength. However, this substance is illegal and produces harmful side effects. Premature closure of growth plates in bones can occur if abused by a teenager, limiting adult height. Other effects include bloody cysts in the liver, increased risk of cardiovascular disease, increased blood pressure, and dysfunction of the reproductive system.

Alcohol – This is a legal substance for adults but is very commonly abused. Moderate to excessive consumption can lead to an increased risk of cardiovascular disease, nutritional deficiencies, and dehydration. Alcohol also causes ill effects on various aspects of performance such as reaction time, coordination, accuracy, balance, and strength.

Nicotine – Another legal but often abused substance that can increase the risk of cardiovascular disease, pulmonary disease, and cancers of the mouth. Nicotine consumption through smoking severely hinders athletic performance by compromising lung function. Smoking especially affects performance in endurance activities.

Marijuana – This is the most commonly abused illegal substance. Adverse effects include a loss of focus and motivation, decreased coordination, and lack of concentration.

Cocaine – Another illegal and somewhat commonly abused substance. Effects include increased alertness and excitability. This drug can give the user a sense of over confidence and invincibility, leading to a false sense of one's ability to perform certain activities. A high heart rate is associated with the use of cocaine, leading to an increased risk of heart attack, stroke, potentially deadly arrhythmias, and seizures.

TEACHER CERTIFICATION STUDY GUIDE

ANNOTATED LIST OF RESOURCES FOR PHYSICAL EDUCATION

This list identifies some resources that may help candidates prepare to take the Physical Education examination. While not a substitute for coursework or other types of teacher preparation, these resources may enhance a candidate's knowledge of the content covered on the examination. The references listed are not intended to represent a comprehensive listing of all potential resources. Candidates are not expected to read all of the materials listed below, and passing the examination will not require familiarity with these specific resources. When available, we have provided a brief summary for the reference cited. We have organized the resources alphabetically and by content domain in subtest order.

GROWTH, MOTOR DEVELOPMENT, AND MOTOR LEARNING

Colvin, A. Vonnie; Nancy J.; and Walker, Pamela. (2000). *Teaching the Nuts and Bolts of Physical Education: Building Basic Movement Skills*. Champaign, IL: Human Kinetics.

> Provides foundational content knowledge in locomotor and manipulative skills. Topics include rolling, throwing, catching, passing, dribbling, striking, kicking, and punting.

Fronske, H. (2001). *Teaching Cues for Sports Skills* (2nd edition). San Francisco, CA: Pearson/Cummings.

> Designed to provide verbal and alternate teaching cues and point out common errors in a variety of sports.

Graham, George. (1992). *Teaching Children Physical Education: Becoming a Master Teacher*. Champaign, IL: Human Kinetics.

> Includes the skills and techniques that successful teachers use to make their classes more interesting and developmentally appropriate. A reference for K-5 teachers and physical education department chairs and administrators.

Lawson, H.A. (1984). *Invitation to Physical Education*. Champaign IL: Human Kinetics.

> Shows students and practitioners how to apply basic business management principles to a variety of health promotion programs.

Pangrazi, Robert. (2004). *Dynamic Physical Education for Elementary School Children* (14th edition). San Francisco, CA: Pearson/Cummings.

> Provides step-by-step techniques for teaching physical education while navigating through today's challenging educational terrain.

Powers, S.K., and Howley, E.T. (2003). *Exercise Physiology* (5th edition). New York, NY: McGraw Hill.

> Explains theory of exercise science and physical education with application and performance models to increase understanding of classroom learning.

Schmidt, R.A., and Lee, T.D. (1999). *Motor Control Learning: A Behavioral Emphasis* (3rd Edition). Champaign: IL: Human Kinetics.

> Addresses many factors that affect the quality of movement behaviors and the ease with which students can learn them.

Sherrill, C. (1998). *Adapted Physical Activity, Recreation and Sport: Cross-disciplinary and Lifespan* (5th edition). Dubuque, IA: WCB McGraw Hill.
> Emphasizes attitude change, inclusion, and psychosocial perspectives for understanding individual differences.

Siedentop, D. (1994). *Sport Education.* Champaign, IL: Human Kinetics.
> Shows how sport can help students learn fair play, leadership skills, and self-responsibility, in addition to becoming competent players. Also shows physical educators how to implement effective sport education programs to achieve these goals.

Summers, J.J. (1992). *Approaches to the Study of Motor Control and Learning.* Amsterdam: Elsevier Science.
> Provides analysis of research with particular emphasis on the methods and paradigms employed and the future direction of their work.

Thomas, Katherine, et al. (2003). *Physical Education Methods for Elementary Teachers.* Champaign, IL: Human Kinetics.
> Takes a research approach and offers a user-friendly technique to applicable teaching modalities for physical education for grades K-12.

Winnick, J.P. (2000). *Adapted Physical Education and Sport* (3rd edition). Champaign, IL: Human Kinetics.
> Provides a thorough introduction for students preparing to work with individuals with disabilities in a variety of settings.

THE SCIENCE OF HUMAN MOVEMENT

Birrell, S., and Cole, C.L. (1994). *Women, Sport, and Culture.* Champaign, IL: Human Kinetics.
> A collection of essays that examine the relationship between sport and gender.

Grantham, W.C.; Patton, R.W.; Winick, M.L.; and York, T.D. (1998). *Health Fitness Management.* Champaign, IL: Human Kinetics.
> Brings conventional business management principles and operational guidelines to the unconventional business of health and fitness.

Hall, S. (2003). *Basic Biomechanics.* Boston, MA: McGraw-Hill.

Hamill, J., and Knutzen, K. (1995). *Biomechanical Basis of Human Movement.* Hagerstown, MD: Lippincott, Williams & Wilkins.
> Integrates aspects of functional anatomy, physics, calculus, and physiology into a comprehensive discussion of human movement.

Hopper, Chris; Fisher, Bruce; and Muniz, Kathy. (1997). *Health-Related Fitness: Grades 1-2, 3-4, 5-6.* Champaign, IL: Human Kinetics.
> These three books provide a wealth of health and fitness information and are an excellent resource for classroom teachers with limited backgrounds in physical education.

Lawson, H.A. (1984). *Invitation to Physical Education.* Champaign, IL: Human Kinetics.
> Shows students and practitioners how to apply basic business management principles to a variety of health promotion programs.

Sample Test

1. The physical education philosophy based on experience is: (Average Rigor) (Skill 1.1)

   A. Naturalism

   B. Pragmatism

   C. Idealism

   D. Existentialism

2. Idealism believes in: (Rigorous) (Skill 1.1)

   A. The laws of nature

   B. Experience is the key

   C. Practice, practice, practice

   D. The mind is developed through acquisition of knowledge

3. Which of the following is not a skill assessment test to evaluate student performance? (Average Rigor) (Skill 1.1)

   A. Harrocks Volley

   B. Rodgers Strength Test

   C. Iowa Brace Test

   D. AAHPERD Youth Fitness Test

4. All of the following are methods to evaluate the affective domain except: (Average Rigor) (Skill 1.1)

   A. Adams Prosocial Inventory

   B. Crowell Personal Distance Scale

   C. Blanchard Behavior Rating Scale

   D. McCloy's Prosocial Behavior Scale

5. Educators can evaluate the cognitive domain by all of the following methods except: (Rigorous) (Skill 1.1)

   A. Norm-Referenced Tests

   B. Criterion Referenced Tests

   C. Standardized Tests

   D. Willis Sports Inventory Tests

6. Using the same foot to take off from a surface and land is which locomotor skill? (Easy) (Skill 1.1)

   A. Jumping

   B. Vaulting

   C. Leaping

   D. Hopping

PHYSICAL EDUCATION

7. Which nonlocomotor skill entails movement around a joint where two body parts meet? (Easy) (Skill 1.1)

   A. Twisting

   B. Swaying

   C. Bending

   D. Stretching

8. A sharp change of direction from one's original line of movement is which nonlocomotor skill? (Easy) (Skill 1.1)

   A. Twisting

   B. Dodging

   C. Swaying

   D. Swinging

9. Which movement concept involves students making decisions about an object's positional changes in space? (Rigorous) (Skill 1.1)

   A. Spatial Awareness

   B. Effort Awareness

   C. Body Awareness

   D. Motion Awareness

10. Applying the mechanical principles of balance, time, and force describes which movement concept? (Average Rigor) (Skill 1.1)

    A. Spatial Awareness

    B. Effort Awareness

    C. Body Awareness

    D. Motion Awareness

11. Having students move on their hands and knees, move on lines, and/or hold shapes while moving develops which quality of movement? (Average Rigor) (Skill 1.1)

    A. Balance

    B. Time

    C. Force

    D. Inertia

12. **What is the proper order of sequential development for the acquisition of locomotor skills? (Rigorous) (Skill 1.1)**

    A. Creep, crawl, walk, jump, run, slide, gallop, hop, leap, skip; step-hop.

    B. Crawl, walk, creep, slide, walk, run, hop, leap, gallop, skip; step-hop.

    C. Creep, crawl, walk, slide, run, hop, leap, skip, gallop, jump; step-hop.

    D. Crawl, creep, walk, run, jump, hop, gallop, slide, leap, skip; step-hop.

13. **Having students pretend they are playing basketball or trying to catch a bus develops which locomotor skill? (Easy) (Skill 1.1)**

    A. Galloping

    B. Running

    C. Leaping

    D. Skipping

14. **Having students play Fox and Hound develops: (Easy) (Skill 1.1)**

    A. Galloping

    B. Hopping

    C. Stepping-hopping

    D. Skipping

15. **Having students take off and land with both feet together develops which locomotor skill? (Easy) (Skill 1.1)**

    A. Hopping

    B. Jumping

    C. Leaping

    D. Skipping

16. **What is the proper sequential order of development for the acquisition of nonlocomotor skills? (Average Rigor) (Skill 1.1)**

    A. Stretch, sit, bend, turn, swing, twist, shake, rock & sway, dodge; fall.

    B. Bend, stretch, turn, twist, swing, sit, rock & sway, shake, dodge; fall.

    C. Stretch, bend, sit, shake, turn, rock & sway, swing, twist, dodge; fall.

    D. Bend, stretch, sit, turn, twist, swing, sway, rock & sway, dodge; fall.

17. Activities such as pretending to pick fruit off a tree or reaching for a star develop which non-locomotor skill? (Easy) (Skill 1.1)

    A. Bending

    B. Stretching

    C. Turning

    D. Twisting

18. Picking up coins, tying shoes, and petting animals develop this nonlocomotor skill. (Easy) (Skill 1.1)

    A. Bending

    B. Stretching

    C. Turning

    D. Twisting

19. Having students collapse in their own space or lower themselves as though they are a raindrop or snowflake develops this nonlocomotor skill. (Easy) (Skill 1.1)

    A. Dodging

    B. Shaking

    C. Swinging

    D. Falling

20. Which is the proper sequential order of development for the acquisition of manipulative skills? (Rigorous) (Skill 1.1)

    A. Striking, throwing, bouncing, catching, trapping, kicking, ball rolling; volleying.

    B. Striking, throwing, kicking, ball rolling, volleying, bouncing, catching; trapping.

    C. Striking, throwing, catching, trapping, kicking, ball rolling, bouncing; volleying.

    D. Striking, throwing, kicking, ball rolling, bouncing; volleying.

21. Having students hit a large balloon with both hands develops this manipulative skill. (Average Rigor) (Skill 1.1)

    A. Bouncing

    B. Striking

    C. Volleying

    D. Trapping

22. Progressively decreasing the size of a target that balls are projected at develops which manipulative skill. (Average Rigor) (Skill 1.1)

    A. Throwing

    B. Trapping

    C. Volleying

    D. Kicking

23. Hitting a stationary object while in a fixed position, then incorporating movement, develops this manipulative skill. (Average Rigor) (Skill 1.1)

    A. Bouncing

    B. Trapping

    C. Throwing

    D. Striking

24. Which of the following body types is the most capable of motor performance involving endurance? (Average Rigor) (Skill 1.2)

    A. Endomorph

    B. Ectomorph

    C. Mesomorph

    D. Metamorph

25. Which of the following countries did not greatly influence the early development of P.E. in the States: (Easy) (Skill 2.1)

    A. Germany

    B. England

    C. Norway

    D. Sweden

26. What was the first state in the U.S. to require P.E. in its public schools? (Average Rigor) (Skill 2.1)

    A. Florida

    B. Massachusetts

    C. New York

    D. California

27. President Eisenhower was alerted to the poor fitness levels of American youths. How was the poor physical conditioning of youths discovered in the Eisenhower Administration? (Average Rigor) (Skill 2.1)

   A. By WWII Selective Service Examination

   B. By organizations promoting physical fitness

   C. By the Federal Security Agency

   D. By the Kraus-Webber Tests

28. In 1956, the AAHPER Fitness Conferences established: (Rigorous) (Skill 2.1)

   A. The President's Council on Youth Fitness

   B. The President's Citizens' Advisory Committee

   C. The President's Council on Physical Fitness

   D. A and B

29. Students that paddle balls against a wall or jump over objects with various heights are demonstrating which quality of movement? (Rigorous) (Skill 2.1)

   A. Balance

   B. Time

   C. Force

   D. Inertia

30. All of the following affect force except: (Easy) (Skill 2.1)

   A. Magnitude

   B. Energy

   C. Motion

   D. Mass

31. For a movement to occur, applied force must overcome inertia of an object and any other resisting forces. What concept of force does this describe? (Rigorous)(Skill 2.1)

   A. Potential energy

   B. Magnitude

   C. Kinetic energy

   D. Absorption

32. The energy of an object to do work while recoiling is which type of potential energy? (Average Rigor) (Skill 2.1)

    A. Absorption

    B. Kinetic

    C. Elastic

    D. Torque

33. Gradually decelerating a moving mass by utilization of smaller forces over a long period of time is: (Average Rigor) (Skill 2.1)

    A. Stability

    B. Equilibrium

    C. Angular force

    D. Force absorption

34. Which of the following principles is not a factor to assess or correct errors in performance for process assessment? (Average Rigor) (Skill 2.1)

    A. Inertia

    B. Action/Reaction

    C. Force

    D. Acceleration

35. An instructor used a similar movement from a skill learned in a different activity to teach a skill for a new activity. The technique used to facilitate cognitive learning was: (Rigorous) (Skill 2.1)

    A. Conceptual thinking

    B. Transfer of learning

    C. Longer instruction

    D. Appropriate language

36. A teacher rewards students for completing tasks. Which method is the teacher using to facilitate psychomotor learning? (Average Rigor) (Skill 2.1)

    A. Task/Reciprocal

    B. Command/Direct

    C. Contingency/Contract

    D. Physical/Reflex

37. The Round Hill School (a private school) in Massachusetts was the first school to require P.E. in its curriculum. What year was this? (Average Rigor) (Skill 2.1)

    A. 1792

    B. 1823

    C. 1902

    D. 1806

38. All of the following are Systematic Observational Evaluations except: (Rigorous) (Skill 2.3)

   A. Reflective Recording

   B. Event Recording

   C. Duration Recording

   D. Self Recording

39. What year did California enact a law requiring all public schools to include physical education in its curriculum: (Easy) (Skill 2.1)

   A. 1892

   B. 1866

   C. 1901

   D. 1899

40. Title IX ensured that: (Easy) (Skill 3.1)

   A. Boys play baseball while girls play softball

   B. Girls are ensured the same educational and athletic opportunities as boys

   C. Girls and boys have coed physical education classes

   D. All students must dress out for physical education class

41. Through physical activities, John has developed self-discipline, fairness, respect for others, and new friends. John has experienced which of the following? (Rigorous) (Skill 3.1)

   A. Positive cooperation psycho-social influences

   B. Positive group psycho-social influences

   C. Positive individual psycho-social influences

   D. Positive accomplishment psycho-social influences

42. Which of the following psycho-social influences is not considered negative? (Rigorous) (Skill 3.1)

   A. Avoidance of problems

   B. Adherence to exercise

   C. Ego-centeredness

   D. Role conflict

43. The affective domain of physical education contributes to all of the following except: (Rigorous) (Skill 3.1)

   A. Knowledge of exercise, health, and disease

   B. Self-actualization

   C. An appreciation of beauty

   D. Good sportsmanship

44. A physical education instructor anticipates and prevents potential injuries, watches for hidden injuries, and takes an injury evaluation of the entire class. Which of the following strategies to prevent injuries is the teacher demonstrating? (Average Rigor) (Skill 3.1)

   A. Maintaining hiring standards

   B. Proper use of equipment

   C. Proper procedures for emergencies

   D. Participant screening

45. An instructor notices that class participation is much lower than expected. By making changes in equipment and rules, the instructor applied which of the following concepts to enhance participation? (Rigorous) (Skill 3.1)

   A. Homogeneous grouping

   B. Heterogeneous grouping

   C. Multi-activity designs

   D. Activity modification

46. Using tactile clues is a functional adaptation that can assist which type of students? (Rigorous) (Skill 3.1)

   A. Deaf students

   B. Blind students

   C. Asthmatic students

   D. Physically challenged students

47. There are two sequential phases to the development of spatial awareness. What is the order of these phases? (Rigorous) (Skill 3.1)

   A. Locating more than one object in relation to each object; the location of objects in relation to one's own body in space.

   B. The location of objects in relation to one's own body in space; locating more than one object in relation to one's own body.

   C. Locating more than one object independent of one's body; the location of objects in relation to one's own body.

   D. The location of objects in relation to one's own body in space; locating more than one object in relation to each object and independent of one's own body.

48. Equilibrium is maintained as long as: (Average Rigor) (Skill 3.1)

    A. Body segments are moved independently.

    B. The center of gravity is over the base of support

    C. Force is applied to the base of support.

    D. The center of gravity is lowered.

49. Which of the following does not enhance equilibrium? (Average Rigor) (Skill 3.1)

    A. Shifting the center of gravity away from the direction of movement.

    B. Increasing the base of support.

    C. Lowering the base of support.

    D. Increasing the base of support and lowering the center of support.

50. The most effective way to promote the physical education curriculum is to: (Rigorous) (Skill 3.2)

    A. Relate physical education to higher thought processes

    B. Relate physical education to humanitarianism

    C. Relate physical education to the total educational process

    D. Relate physical education to skills necessary to preserve the natural environment

51. Which of the following is not a consideration for the selection of a facility? (Rigorous) (Skill 3.2)

    A. Community involvement

    B. Custodial staff

    C. Availability to women, minorities, and the handicapped

    D. Bond issues

52. Which of the following is not a class-management technique? (Easy) (Skill 3.2)

   A. Explaining procedures for roll call, excuses, and tardiness

   B. Explaining routines for changing and showering

   C. Explaining conditioning

   D. Promoting individual self-discipline

53. Long-term planning is essential for effective class management. Identify the management techniques not essential to long-term planning. (Easy) (Skill 3.2)

   A. Parental observation

   B. Progress evaluation

   C. Precise activity planning

   D. Arrangements for line markings

54. Although Mary is a paraplegic, she wants to participate in some capacity in the physical education class. What federal legislative act entitles her to do so? (Rigorous) (Skill 3.2)

   A. PE 94-142

   B. Title IX

   C. PL 94-142

   D. Title XI

55. A legal wrong resulting in a direct or an indirect injury is: (Average Rigor) (Skill 3.2)

   A. Negligence

   B. A Tort

   C. In loco parentis

   D. Legal liability

56. All of the following actions help avoid lawsuits except: (Average Rigor) (Skill 3.2)

   A. Ensuring equipment and facilities are safe

   B. Getting exculpatory agreements

   C. Knowing each students' health status

   D. Grouping students with unequal competitive levels

57. Which of the following actions does not promote safety? (Rigorous) (Skill 3.2)

   A. Allowing students to wear the current style of shoes

   B. Presenting organized activities

   C. Inspecting equipment and facilities

   D. Instructing skill and activities properly

58. The tendency of a body/object to remain in its present state of motion unless some force acts to change it is which mechanical principle of motion? (Average Rigor)(Skill 3.2)

   A. Acceleration

   B. Inertia

   C. Action/Reaction

   D. Linear motion

59. The movement response of a system depends not only on the net external force, but also on the resistance to movement change. Which mechanical principle of motion does this definition describe? (Rigorous) (Skill 3.2)

   A. Acceleration

   B. Inertia

   C. Action/Reaction

   D. Air Resistance

60. Which of the following mechanical principles of motion states that every motion has a similar, contrasting response? (Easy) (Skill 3.2)

   A. Acceleration

   B. Inertia

   C. Action/Reaction

   D. Centripetal force

61. A subjective, observational approach to identifying errors in the form, style, or mechanics of a skill is accomplished by: (Rigorous) (Skill 4.1)

   A. Product assessment

   B. Process assessment

   C. Standardized norm-referenced tests

   D. Criterion-referenced tests

62. What type of assessment objectively measures skill performance? (Rigorous) (Skill 4.1)

   A. Process assessment

   B. Product assessment

   C. Texas PE Test

   D. Iowa Brace Test

63. Process assessment does not identify which of the following errors in skill performance. (Average Rigor) (Skill 4.1)

    A. Style

    B. Form

    C. End result

    D. Mechanics

64. Determining poor performance of a skill using process assessment can best be accomplished by: (Average Rigor) (Skill 4.1)

    A. Observing how fast a skill is performed.

    B. Observing how many skills are performed.

    C. Observing how far or how high a skill is performed.

    D. Observing several attributes comprising the entire performance of a skill.

65. Which of the following methods measures fundamental skills using product assessment? (Rigorous) (Skill 4.1)

    A. Criterion-referenced tests

    B. Standardized norm-referenced tests

    C. Both A and B

    D. Neither A nor B

66. Product assessment measures all of the following except: (Rigorous) (Skill 4.1)

    A. How the student performs the mechanics of a skill.

    B. How many times the student performs a skill.

    C. How fast the student performs a skill.

    D. How far or high the student performs a skill.

67. Instructors can evaluate skill level of achievement in archery by: (Average Rigor) (Skill 4.1)

    A. Giving students a written exam on terminology.

    B. Having students demonstrate the correct tension of arrow feathers.

    C. Totaling a student's score obtained on the target's face.

    D. Time how long a student takes to shoot all arrows.

68. Instructors can determine skill level achievement in golf by: (Average Rigor) (Skill 4.1)

   A. The number of "birdies" that a student makes.

   B. The number of "bogies" a student makes.

   C. The score obtained after several rounds

   D. The total score achieved throughout the school year.

69. Instructors can determine skill level achievement in swimming by: (Average Rigor) (Skill 4.1)

   A. How long a student can float

   B. How many strokes it takes a student to swim a specified distance.

   C. How long a student can stay under the water without moving.

   D. How many times a student can dive in five minutes.

70. Instructors can assess skill level achievement in bowling by: (Easy) (Skill 4.1)

   A. Calculating a student's average score.

   B. Calculating how many gutter-balls the student threw.

   C. Calculating how many strikes the student threw.

   D. Calculating how many spares the student threw.

71. Although they are still hitting the target, the score of some students practicing archery has decreased as the distance between them and the target has increased. Which of the following adjustments will improve their scores? (Rigorous) (Skill 4.1)

   A. Increasing the velocity of their arrows.

   B. Increasing the students' base of support.

   C. Increasing the weight of the arrows.

   D. Increasing the parabolic path of the arrows.

72. Some students practicing basketball are having difficulty with "free throws," even though the shots make it to and over the hoop. What adjustment will improve their "free throws"?
(Average Rigor) (Skill 4.1)

   A. Increasing the height of release (i.e. jump shot).

   B. Increasing the vertical path of the ball.

   C. Increasing the velocity of the release.

   D. Increasing the base of support.

73. An archery student's arrow bounced off the red part of the target face. What is the correct ruling? (Average Rigor) (Skill 4.1)

   A. No score.

   B. Re-shoot arrow.

   C. 7 points awarded.

   D. Shot receives same score as highest arrow shot that did not bounce off the target.

74. A student playing badminton believed that the shuttlecock was going to land out-of-bounds. The shuttlecock landed on the line. What is the correct ruling? (Easy) (Skill 4.1)

   A. The shuttlecock is out-of-bounds.

   B. The shuttlecock is in-bounds.

   C. The point is replayed.

   D. That player is charged with a feint.

75. A mechanical pinsetter accidentally knocked down the only bowling pin left standing for a spare attempt after clearing all the other pins knocked down by the first ball thrown. What is the correct ruling? (Rigorous) (Skill 4.1)

   A. Foul

   B. Spare

   C. Frame is replayed

   D. No count for that pin

76. The ball served in racquetball hits the front line and lands in front of the short line. What is the ruling? (Easy) (Skill 4.1)

    A. Fault

    B. Reserve

    C. Out-of-bounds

    D. Fair ball

77. Two opposing soccer players are trying to gain control of the ball when one player "knees" the other. What is the ruling? (Easy) (Skill 4.1)

    A. Direct free kick

    B. Indirect free kick

    C. Fair play

    D. Ejection from the game

78. Two students are playing badminton. When receiving the shuttlecock, one student consistently stands too deep in the receiving court. What strategy should the server use to serve the shuttlecock? (Average Rigor) (Skill 4.1)

    A. Smash serve

    B. Clear serve

    C. Overhead serve

    D. Short serve

79. A basketball team has an outstanding rebounder. In order to keep this player near the opponent's basket, which strategy should the coach implement? (Easy) (Skill 4.1)

    A. Pick-and-Roll

    B. Give-and-Go

    C. Zone defense

    D. Free-lancing

80. When a defensive tennis player needs more time to return to his position, what strategy should he apply? (Rigorous) (Skill 4.1)

    A. Drop shot

    B. Dink shot

    C. Lob shot

    D. Down-the-line shot

81. An overhead badminton stroke used to hit a fore-hand-like overhead stroke that is on the backhand side of the body is called: (Rigorous) (Skill 4.1)

    A. Around-the-head-shot

    B. Down-the-line shot

    C. Lifting the shuttle

    D. Under hand shuttle

82. A maneuver when an offensive player passes to a teammate and then immediately cuts in toward the basket for a return pass is: (Average Rigor) (Skill 4.1)

   A. Charging

   B. Pick

   C. Give-and-go

   D. Switching

83. A bowling pin that remains standing after an apparently perfect hit is called a: (Rigorous) (Skill 4.1)

   A. Tap

   B. Turkey

   C. Blow

   D. Leave

84. A soccer pass from the outside of the field near the end line to a position in front of the goal is called: (Average Rigor) (Skill 4.1)

   A. Chip

   B. Settle

   C. Through

   D. Cross

85. A volleyball that is simultaneously contacted above the net by opponents and momentarily held upon contact is called a/an: (Easy) (Skill 4.1)

   A. Double fault

   B. Play over

   C. Overlap

   D. Held ball

86. Volleyball player LB on team A digs a spiked ball. The ball deflects off of LB's shoulder. What is the ruling? (Average Rigor) (Skill 4.1)

   A. Fault

   B. Legal hit

   C. Double foul

   D. Play over

87. Playing "Simon Says" and having students touch different body parts applies which movement concept? (Average Rigor) (Skill 4.2)

   A. Spatial Awareness

   B. Effort Awareness

   C. Body Awareness

   D. Motion Awareness

88. Having students move in a specific pattern while measuring how long they take to do so develops which quality of movement? (Average Rigor) (Skill 4.2)

    A. Balance

    B. Time

    C. Force

    D. Inertia

89. Aerobic dance develops or improves each of the following skills or health components except... (Rigorous) (Skill 4.2)

    A. Cardio-respiratory function

    B. Body composition

    C. Coordination

    D. Flexibility

90. Rowing develops which health or skill related component of fitness? (Rigorous) (Skill 4.2)

    A. Muscle endurance

    B. Flexibility

    C. Balance

    D. Reaction time

91. Calisthenics develops all of the following health and skill related components of fitness except: (Average Rigor) (Skill 4.2)

    A. Muscle strength

    B. Body composition

    C. Power

    D. Agili

92. Which health or skill related components of fitness are developed by rope jumping? (Average Rigor) (Skill 4.2)

    A. Muscle Force

    B. Coordination

    C. Flexibility

    D. Muscle strength

93. Swimming does not improve which health or skill related component of fitness? (Rigorous) (Skill 4.2)

    A. Cardio-respiratory function

    B. Flexibility

    C. Muscle strength

    D. Foot Speed

94. Data from a cardio-respiratory assessment can identify and predict all of the following except: (Rigorous) (Skill 4.2)

    A. Functional aerobic capacity

    B. Natural over-fatness

    C. Running ability

    D. Motivation

95. Data from assessing _____ identifies an individual's potential of developing musculoskeletal problems and an individual's potential of performing activities of daily living. (Rigorous) (Skill 4.2)

    A. Flexibility

    B. Muscle endurance

    C. Muscle strength

    D. Motor performance

96. A 17-year-old male student performed 20 sit-ups, ran a mile in 8 minutes, and has a body fat composition of 17%. Which is the best interpretation of his fitness level? (Rigorous) (Skill 4.2)

    A. Average muscular endurance, good cardiovascular endurance; appropriate body fat composition.

    B. Low muscular endurance, average cardiovascular endurance; high body fat composition.

    C. Low muscular endurance, average cardiovascular endurance; appropriate body fat composition.

    D. Low muscular endurance, low cardiovascular endurance; appropriate body fat composition.

97. Based on the information given in the previous question, what changes would you recommend to improve this person's level of fitness? (Average Rigor) (Skill 4.2)

   A. Muscle endurance training and cardiovascular endurance training.

   B. Muscle endurance training, cardiovascular endurance training, and reduction of caloric intake.

   C. Muscle strength training and cardio-vascular endurance training.

   D. No changes necessary.

98. An obese student's fitness assessments were poor for every component of fitness. Which would you recommend first? (Easy) (Skill 4.2)

   A. A jogging program.

   B. A weight lifting program.

   C. A walking program.

   D. A stretching program.

99. Coordinated movements that project a person over an obstacle are known as: (Easy) (Skill 4.4)

   A. Jumping

   B. Vaulting

   C. Leaping

   D. Hopping

100. Which manipulative skill uses the hands to stop the momentum of an object? (Rigorous) (Skill 4.4)

   A. Trapping

   B. Catching

   C. Striking

   D. Rolling

101. Which professional organization protects amateur sports from corruption? (Easy) (Skill 5.2)

   A. AIWA

   B. AAHPERD

   C. NCAA

   D. AAU

102. Which professional organization works with legislatures? (Average Rigor) (Skill 5.1)

   A. AIWA

   B. AAHPERD

   C. ACSM

   D. AAU

103. Research in physical education is published in all of the following periodicals except the: (Average Rigor) (Skill 5.1)

   A. School PE Update

   B. Research Quarterly

   C. Journal of Physical Education

   D. YMCA Magazine

104. A teacher who modifies and develops tasks for a class is demonstrating knowledge of which appropriate behavior in physical education activities? (Rigorous) (Skill 5.1)

   A. Appropriate management behavior

   B. Appropriate student behavior

   C. Appropriate administration behavior

   D. Appropriate content behavior

105. The ability for a muscle(s) to repeatedly contract over a period of time is: (Average Rigor) (Skill 5.1)

   A. Cardiovascular endurance

   B. Muscle endurance

   C. Muscle strength

   D. Muscle force

106. The ability to change rapidly the direction of the body is: (Average Rigor) (Skill 5.1)

   A. Coordination

   B. Reaction time

   C. Speed

   D. Agility

107. Students are performing the vertical jump. What component of fitness does this activity assess? (Rigorous) (Skill 5.1)

   A. Muscle strength

   B. Balance

   C. Power

   D. Muscle endurance

108. Using the Karvonen Formula, compute the 60% - 80% THR for a 16-year old student with a RHR of 60. (Rigorous) (Skill 5.1)

    A. 122-163 beats per minute

    B. 130-168 beats per minute

    C. 142-170 beats per minute

    D. 146-175 beats per minute

109. Using Cooper's Formula, compute the THR for a 15 year old student. (Rigorous) (Skill 5.1)

    A. 120- 153 beats per minute

    B. 123-164 beats per minute

    C. 135-169 beats per minute

    D. 147-176 beats per minute

110. Which is not a common negative stressor? (Rigorous) (Skill 5.1)

    A. Loss of significant other

    B. Personal illness or injury.

    C. Moving to a new state.

    D. Landing a new job.

111. Which of the following is a negative coping strategy for dealing with stress? (Average Rigor) (Skill 5.1)

    A. Recreational diversions

    B. Active thinking

    C. Alcohol use

    D. Imagery

112. The most important nutrient the body requires, without which life can only be sustained for a few days, is: (Easy) (Skill 5.1)

    A. Vitamins

    B. Minerals

    C. Water

    D. Carbohydrates

113. With regard to protein content, foods from animal sources are usually: (Average Rigor) (Skill 5.1)

    A. Complete

    B. Essential

    C. Nonessential

    D. Incidental

114. Fats with room for two or more hydrogen atoms per molecule-fatty acid chain are: (Rigorous) (Skill 5.1)

   A. Monounsaturated

   B. Polyunsaturated

   C. Hydrosaturated

   D. Saturated

115. An adequate diet to meet nutritional needs consists of: (Rigorous) (Skill 5.1)

   A. No more than 30% caloric intake from fats, no more than 50 % caloric intake from proteins, and at least 20% caloric intake from carbohydrates.

   B. No more than 30% caloric intake from fats, no more than 40% caloric intake from proteins, and at least 30% caloric intake from carbohydrates.

   C. No more than 30% caloric intake from fats, no more than 15% caloric intake from proteins, and at least 55% caloric intake from carbohydrates.

   D. No more than 30 % caloric intake from fats, no more than 30% caloric intake from proteins, and at least 40% caloric intake from carbohydrates.

116. Maintaining body weight is best accomplished by: (Average Rigor) (Skill 5.1)

   A. Dieting

   B. Aerobic exercise

   C. Lifting weights

   D. Equalizing caloric intake relative to output

117. Most high-protein diets: (Average Rigor) (Skill 5.1)

   A. Are high in cholesterol

   B. Are high in saturated fats

   C. Require vitamin and mineral supplements

   D. All of the above

118. Which one of the following statements about low-calorie diets is false? (Rigorous) (Skill 5.1)

   A. Most people who "diet only" regain the weight they lose.

   B. They are the way most people try to lose weight.

   C. They make weight control easier.

   D. They lead to excess worry about weight, food, and eating.

119. Physiological benefits of exercise include all of the following except: (Average Rigor) (Skill 5.1)

   A. Reducing mental tension

   B. Improving muscle strength

   C. Cardiac hypertrophy

   D. Quicker recovery rate

120. Psychological benefits of exercise include all of the following except: (Rigorous) (Skill 5.1)

   A. Improved sleeping patterns

   B. Improved energy regulation

   C. Improved appearance

   D. Improved quality of life

121. Which of the following conditions is not associated with a lack of physical activity? (Average Rigor) (Skill 5.1)

   A. Atherosclerosis

   B. Longer life expectancy

   C. Osteoporosis

   D. Certain cancers

122. Which of the following pieces of exercise equipment best applies the physiological principles? (Average Rigor) (5.1)

   A. Rolling machine

   B. Electrical muscle stimulator

   C. Stationary Bicycle

   D. Motor-driven rowing machine

123. To enhance skill and strategy performance for striking or throwing objects, for catching or collecting objects, and for carrying and propelling objects, students must first learn techniques for: (Rigorous) (Skill 5.3)

   A. Offense

   B. Defense

   C. Controlling objects

   D. Continuous play of objects

124. Which of the following is not a type of tournament? (Average Rigor) (Skill 5.3)

   A. Spiderweb

   B. Pyramid

   C. Spiral

   D. Round Robin

125. Which of the following is not a type of meet? (Average Rigor) (Skill 5.3)

   A. Extramural

   B. Intramural

   C. Interscholastic

   D. Ladder

126. Activities to specifically develop cardiovascular fitness must be: (Rigorous) (Skill 6.1)

   A. Performed without developing an oxygen debt

   B. Performed twice daily.

   C. Performed every day.

   D. Performed for a minimum of 10 minutes.

127. Which is not a sign of stress? (Average Rigor) (Skill 6.1)

   A. Irritability

   B. Assertiveness

   C. Insomnia

   D. Stomach problems

128. Students are performing trunk extensions. What component of fitness does this activity assess? (Average Rigor) (Skill 9.1)

   A. Balance

   B. Flexibility

   C. Body Composition

   D. Coordination

129. Working at a level that is above normal is which exercise training principle? (Rigorous) (Skill 9.1)

   A. Intensity

   B. Progression

   C. Specificity

   D. Overload

130. Students on a running program to improve cardio-respiratory fitness apply which exercise principle? (Rigorous) (Skill 9.1)

   A. Aerobic

   B. Progression

   C. Specificity

   D. Overload

131. Adding more reps to a weightlifting set applies which exercise principle? (Average Rigor) (Skill 9.1)

   A. Anaerobic

   B. Progression

   C. Overload

   D. Specificity

132. Which of the following does not modify overload? (Rigorous) (Skill 9.1)

   A. Frequency

   B. Perceived exertion

   C. Time

   D. Intensity

133. Prior to activity, students perform a 5-10 minute warm-up. Which is not recommended as part of the warm-up? (Easy) (Skill 9.1)

   A. Using the muscles that will be utilized in the following activity.

   B. Using a gradual aerobic warm-up.

   C. Using a gradual anaerobic warm-up.

   D. Stretching the major muscle groups to be used in the activity.

134. **Which is not a benefit of warming up? (Rigorous) (Skill 9.1)**

   A. Releasing hydrogen from myoglobin.

   B. Reducing the risk of musculoskeletal injuries.

   C. Raising the body's core temperature in preparation for activity.

   D. Stretching the major muscle groups to be used in the activity.

135. **Which is not a benefit of cooling down? (Rigorous) (Skill 9.1)**

   A. Preventing dizziness.

   B. Redistributing circulation.

   C. Removing lactic acid.

   D. Removing myoglobin.

136. **Overloading for muscle strength includes all of the following except: (Rigorous) (Skill 9.1)**

   A. Raising heart rate to an intense level.

   B. Lifting weights every other day.

   C. Lifting with high resistance and low reps.

   D. Lifting 60% to 90% of assessed muscle strength.

137. **Which of the following applies the concept of progression? (Rigorous) (Skill 9.1)**

   A. Beginning a stretching program every day.

   B. Beginning a stretching program with 3 sets of reps.

   C. Beginning a stretching program with ballistic stretching.

   D. Beginning a stretching program holding stretches for 15 seconds and work up to holding stretches for 60 seconds.

138. **Which of following overload principles does not apply to improving body composition? (Average Rigor) (Skill 9.1)**

   A. Aerobic exercise three times per week.

   B. Aerobic exercise at a low intensity.

   C. Aerobic exercise for about an hour.

   D. Aerobic exercise in intervals of high intensity.

139. Which of the following principles of progression applies to improving muscle endurance? (Average Rigor) (Skill 9.1)

A. Lifting weights every day.

B. Lifting weights at 20% to 30% of assessed muscle strength.

C. Lifting weights with low resistance and low reps.

D. Lifting weights starting at 60% of assessed muscle strength.

Answer Key

1.	B	45.	D	89.	D	133.	C
2.	D	46.	B	90.	A	134.	A
3.	A	47.	D	91.	C	135.	D
4.	D	48.	B	92.	B	136.	A
5.	D	49.	A	93.	D	137.	D
6.	D	50.	C	94.	B	138.	A
7.	C	51.	A	95.	A	139.	B
8.	B	52.	C	96.	C		
9.	A	53.	A	97.	A		
10.	B	54.	C	98.	C		
11.	A	55.	B	99.	B		
12.	D	56.	D	100.	B		
13.	B	57.	A	101.	D		
14.	A	58.	B	102.	B		
15.	B	59.	A	103.	A		
16.	C	60.	C	104.	D		
17.	B	61.	B	105.	B		
18.	A	62.	B	106.	D		
19.	D	63.	C	107.	C		
20.	B	64.	D	108.	D		
21.	C	65.	C	109.	B		
22.	A	66.	A	110.	D		
23.	D	67.	C	111.	C		
24.	B	68.	C	112.	C		
25.	C	69.	B	113.	A		
26.	D	70.	A	114.	B		
27.	D	71.	D	115.	C		
28.	D	72.	B	116.	D		
29.	C	73.	C	117.	D		
30.	D	74.	B	118.	C		
31.	B	75.	D	119.	A		
32.	C	76.	A	120.	B		
33.	D	77.	A	121.	B		
34.	C	78.	D	122.	C		
35.	B	79.	C	123.	C		
36.	C	80.	C	124.	C		
37.	B	81.	A	125.	D		
38.	A	82.	C	126.	A		
39.	B	83.	A	127.	B		
40.	B	84.	D	128.	B		
41.	B	85.	D	129.	D		
42.	B	86.	B	130.	C		
43.	A	87.	C	131.	B		
44.	D	88.	B	132.	B		

Rigor Table

Easy %20	Average Rigor %40	Rigorous %40
6,7,8,13, 14, 15, 17, 18,19, 25, 30, 39, 40, 52,53,60, 70, 74, 76, 77, 79, 85, 98, 99, 101, 112, 133	1, 3, 4, 10, 11, 16, 21, 22, 23, 24, 26, 27, 32, 33, 34, 36, 37, 44, 48, 49, 55, 56, 58, 63, 64, 67, 68, 69, 72, 73, 78, 82, 84, 86, 87, 88, 91, 92, 97, 102, 103, 105, 106, 111, 113, 116, 117, 119, 121, 122, 124, 125, 127, 128, 131, 138, 139	2, 5, 9, 12, 20, 28, 29, 31, 35, 38, 41, 42, 43, 45, 46, 47, 50, 51, 54, 57, 59, 61, 62, 65, 66, 71, 75, 80, 81, 83, 89, 90, 93, 94, 95, 96, 100, 104, 107, 108, 109, 110, 114, 115, 118, 120, 123, 126, 129, 130, 132, 134, 135, 136, 137

Rationales with Sample Questions

1. **The physical education philosophy that is based on experience is: (Average Rigor) (Skill 1.1)**
   A. Naturalism
   B. Pragmatism
   C. Idealism
   D. Existentialism

(B.) Pragmatism, as a school of philosophy, is a collection of different ways of thinking. Given the diversity of thinkers and the variety of schools of thought that have adopted this term over the years, the term pragmatism has become almost meaningless in the absence of further qualification. Most of the thinkers who describe themselves as pragmatists indicate some connection with practical consequences or real effects as vital components of both meaning and truth.

2. **Idealism believes in: (Rigorous) (Skill 1.1)**

   A. The laws of nature
   B. Experience is the key
   C. Practice, practice, practice
   D. The mind is developed through acquisition of knowledge

(D.) Idealism believes that the mind continues to develop through the ongoing acquisition of knowledge.

3. **Which of the following is not a skill assessment test to evaluate student performance? (Average Rigor) (Skill 1.1)**
   A. Harrocks Volley
   B. Rodgers Strength Test
   C. Iowa Brace Test
   D. AAHPERD Youth Fitness Test

(A.) Harrocks Volley is a volleyball code for a popular player named James.

4. All of the following are methods to evaluate the affective domain except: (Average Rigor) (Skill 1.1)
   A. Adams Prosocial Inventory
   B. Crowell Personal Distance Scale
   C. Blanchard Behavior Rating Scale
   D. McCloy's Prosocial Behavior Scale

(D.) McCloy's Prosocial Behavior scale provided one of the earliest discussions on the influence of participation in sports and on the development of socially desirable character traits. Not surprisingly, large voids still exist in the knowledge about athletes' moral reasoning. One area that has thus far received little attention by social psychologists is the relationship between sport involvement, moral development, and aggression.

5. Educators can evaluate the cognitive domain by all of the following methods except: (Rigorous) (Skill 1.1)
   A. Norm-Referenced Tests
   B. Criterion Referenced Tests
   C. Standardized Tests
   D. Willis Sports Inventory Tests

(D.) The Willis Sports Inventory Test is the tally of all wins and losses of the popular basketball player, Willis.

6. Using the same foot to take off from a surface and land is which locomotor skill? (Easy) (Skill 1.1)
   A. Jumping
   B. Vaulting
   C. Leaping
   D. Hopping

(D.) Hopping is a move with light, bounding skips or leaps. Basically, it is the ability to jump on one foot.

7. Which nonlocomotor skill entails movement around a joint where two body parts meet? (Easy) (Skill 1.1)
   A. Twisting
   B. Swaying
   C. Bending
   D. Stretching

(C.) Bending is a deviation from a straight-line position. It also means to assume a curved, crooked, or angular form or direction, to incline the body, to make a concession, yield, to apply oneself closely, or to concentrate (e.g., *she bent to her task*).

TEACHER CERTIFICATION STUDY GUIDE

8. A sharp change of direction from one's original line of movement is which nonlocomotor skill? (Easy) (Skill 1.1)
   A. Twisting
   B. Dodging
   C. Swaying
   D. Swinging

(B.) Dodging is the ability to avoid something by moving or shifting quickly aside.

9. Which movement concept involves students making decisions about an object's positional changes in space? (Rigorous) (Skill 1.1)
   A. Spatial Awareness
   B. Effort Awareness
   C. Body Awareness
   D. Motion Awareness

(A.) Spatial awareness is an organized awareness of objects in the space around us. It is also an awareness of our body's position in space. Without this awareness, we would not be able to pick food up from our plates and put it in our mouths. We would have trouble reading, because we will not see the letters in their correct relation to each other and to the page. Athletes would not have the precise awareness of the position of other players on the field and the movement of the ball, which is necessary to play sports effectively.

10. Applying the mechanical principles of balance, time, and force describes which movement concept? (Average Rigor) (Skill 1.1)
    A. Spatial Awareness
    B. Effort Awareness
    C. Body Awareness
    D. Motion Awareness

(B.) Effort Awareness is the knowledge of balance, time, and force and how they relate to athletic movements and activities.

11. Having students move on their hands and knees, move on lines, and/or hold shapes while moving develops which quality of movement? (Average Rigor) (Skill 1.1)
    A. Balance
    B. Time
    C. Force
    D. Inertia

(A.) Balance is one of the physiological senses. It allows humans and animals to walk without falling. Some animals are better at this than humans. For example, a cat (as a quadruped using its inner ear and tail) can walk on a thin fence. All forms of equilbrioception are essentially the detection of acceleration.

PHYSICAL EDUCATION   163

TEACHER CERTIFICATION STUDY GUIDE

12. What is the proper order of sequential development for the acquisition of locomotor skills? (Rigorous) (Skill 1.1)
   A. Creep, crawl, walk, jump, run, slide, gallop, hop, leap, skip; step-hop.
   B. Crawl, walk, creep, slide, walk, run, hop, leap, gallop, skip; step-hop.
   C. Creep, crawl, walk, slide, run, hop, leap, skip, gallop, jump; step-hop.
   D. Crawl, creep, walk, run, jump, hop, gallop, slide, leap, skip; step-hop.

(D.)

LOCOMOTOR SKILL: A skill that utilizes the feet and moves you from one place to another.

CRAWL: A form of locomotion where the person moves in a prone position with the body resting on or close to the ground or on the hands and knees.

CREEP: A slightly more advanced form of locomotion in which the person moves on the hands and knees.

WALK: A form of locomotion in which body weight is transferred alternately from the ball (toe) of one foot to the heel of the other. At times one foot is on the ground and during a brief phase, both feet are on the ground. There is no time when both feet are off the ground.

RUN: A form of locomotion much like the walk except that the tempo and body lean may differ. At times one foot is on the ground and during a brief phase both feet are off the ground. There is no time when both feet are on the ground simultaneously.

JUMP: A form of locomotion in which the body weight is projected from one or two feet and lands on two feet. Basic forms: for height, from height, distance, continuous, and rebounding.

HOP: A form of locomotion in which the body is projected from one foot to the same foot.

GALLOP: A form of locomotion that is a combination of an open step by the leading foot and a closed step by the trailing foot. The same foot leads throughout. The rhythm is uneven.

SLIDE: The same action as the gallop except that the direction of travel is sideways instead of forward. The rhythm is uneven.

LEAP: An exaggerated running step. There is a transfer of weight from one foot to the other and a phase when neither foot is in contact with the ground.

SKIP: A locomotor skill that combines a hop and a step (walk or run). The rhythm is uneven.

PHYSICAL EDUCATION

13. **Having students pretend they are playing basketball or trying to catch a bus develops which locomotor skill? (Easy) (Skill 1.1)**
    A. Galloping
    B. Running
    C. Leaping
    D. Skipping

(**B.**) Playing basketball involves near constant running up and down the court. In addition, chasing is a good example to use with children to illustrate the concept of running.

14. **Having students play Fox and Hound develops: (Easy) (Skill 1.1)**
    A. Galloping
    B. Hopping
    C. Stepping-hopping
    D. Skipping

(**A.**) Fox and Hound is an activity that emphasizes rapid running. The form of the exercise most closely resembles a gallop, especially in rhythm and rapidity. It can develop or progress at an accelerated rate.

15. **Having students take off and land with both feet together develops which locomotor skill? (Easy) (Skill 1.1)**
    A. Hopping
    B. Jumping
    C. Leaping
    D. Skipping

(**B.**) Jumping is a skill that most humans and many animals share. It is the process of getting one's body off of the ground for a short time using one's own power, usually by propelling oneself upward via contraction and then forceful extension of the legs. One can jump up to reach something high, jump over a fence or ditch, or jump down. One can also jump while dancing and as a sport in track and field.

16. **What is the proper sequential order of development for the acquisition of nonlocomotor skills? (Average Rigor) (Skill 1.1)**
    A. Stretch, sit, bend, turn, swing, twist, shake, rock & sway, dodge; fall.
    B. Bend, stretch, turn, twist, swing, sit, rock & sway, shake, dodge; fall.
    C. Stretch, bend, sit, shake, turn, rock & sway, swing, twist, dodge; fall.
    D. Bend, stretch, sit, turn, twist, swing, sway, rock & sway, dodge; fall.

(**C.**) Each skill in the progression builds on the previous skills.

17. Activities such as pretending to pick fruit off a tree or reaching for a star develop which non-locomotor skill? (Easy) (Skill 1.1)
   A. Bending
   B. Stretching
   C. Turning
   D. Twisting

(B.) Stretching is the activity of gradually applying tensile force to lengthen, strengthen, and lubricate muscles, often performed in anticipation of physical exertion and to increase the range of motion within a joint. Stretching is an especially important accompaniment to activities that emphasize controlled muscular strength and flexibility. These include ballet, acrobatics or martial arts. Stretching also may help prevent injury to tendons, ligaments, and muscles by improving muscular elasticity and reducing the stretch reflex in greater ranges of motion that might cause injury to tissue. In addition, stretching can reduce delayed onset muscle soreness (DOMS).

18. Picking up coins, tying shoes, and petting animals develop this nonlocomotor skill. (Easy) (Skill 1.1)
    A. Bending
    B. Stretching
    C. Turning
    D. Twisting

(A.) Bending is the action of moving the body across a skeletal joint. In each of the sample activities, one must bend from the waist or knees to reach a low object.

19. Having students collapse in their own space or lower themselves as if they are a raindrop or snowflake develops this nonlocomotor skill. (Easy) (Skill 1.1)
    A. Dodging
    B. Shaking
    C. Swinging
    D. Falling

(D.) Falling is a major cause of personal injury in athletics. Athletic participants must learn how to fall in such a way as to limit the possibility of injury.

20. **Which is the proper sequential order of development for the acquisition of manipulative skills? (Rigorous) (Skill 1.1)**
    A. Striking, throwing, bouncing, catching, trapping, kicking, ball rolling; volleying.
    B. Striking, throwing, kicking, ball rolling, volleying, bouncing, catching; trapping.
    C. Striking, throwing, catching, trapping, kicking, ball rolling, bouncing; volleying.
    D. Striking, throwing, kicking, ball rolling, bouncing; volleying.

(B.) Striking, throwing, kicking, ball rolling, volleying, bouncing, catching, and trapping is the proper sequential order of development for the acquisition of manipulative skills. Each skill in this progression builds on the previous skill.

21. **Having students hit a large balloon with both hands develops this manipulative skill? (Average Rigor) (Skill 1.1)**
    A. Bouncing
    B. Striking
    C. Volleying
    D. Trapping

(C.) In a number of ball games, a volley is the ball that a player receives and delivers without touching the ground. The ability to volley a ball back and forth requires great body control and spatial awareness.

22. **Progressively decreasing the size of a target that balls are projected at develops which manipulative skill. (Average Rigor) (Skill 1.1)**
    A. Throwing
    B. Trapping
    C. Volleying
    D. Kicking

(A.) Children develop throwing skills (the ability to propel an object through the air with a rapid movement of the arm and wrist) by projecting balls at progressively smaller targets.

23. **Hitting a stationary object while in a fixed position, then incorporating movement, develops this manipulative skill. (Average Rigor) (Skill 1.1)**
    A. Bouncing
    B. Trapping
    C. Throwing
    D. Striking

(D.) Striking is the process of hitting something sharply, with the hand, the fist, or a weapon.

TEACHER CERTIFICATION STUDY GUIDE

24. **Which of the following body types is the most capable of motor performance involving endurance? (Average Rigor) (Skill 1.2)**
    A. Endomorph
    B. Ectomorph
    C. Mesomorph
    D. Metamorph

(B.) Characteristically, ectomorphs are lean and slender with little body fat and musculature. Ectomorphs are usually capable of performing at high levels in endurance events.

25. **Which of the following countries did not greatly influence the early development of P.E. in the States: (Easy) (Skill 1.2)**
    A. Germany
    B. England
    C. Norway
    D. Sweden

(C.) Norway did not have a great influence on the early development of P.E. in the United States.

26. **What was the first state in the U.S. to require P.E. in its public schools? (Average Rigor) (Skill 2.1)**
    A. Florida
    B. Massachusetts
    C. New York
    D. California

(D.) California was the first state in the U.S. to require physical education classes in its public schools curriculum in 1866.

TEACHER CERTIFICATION STUDY GUIDE

27. **President Eisenhower was alerted to the poor fitness levels of American youths. How was the poor physical conditioning of youths discovered in the Eisenhower Administration? (Average Rigor) (Skill 2.1**
   A. By WWII Selective Service Examination
   B. By organizations promoting physical fitness
   C. By the Federal Security Agency
   D. By the Kraus-Webber Tests

(D.) This is one of the programs that President Dwight Eisenhower implemented during his presidency. Using a test devised by Drs. Hans Kraus and Sonja Weber of New York Presbyterian Hospital, Bonnie began testing children in Europe, Central America, and the United States. The Kraus-Weber test involved six simple movements and took 90 seconds to administer. It compared US children to European children in the realms of strength and flexibility. The fitness emphasis in schools started by Kraus-Weber declined in the 1970s and early 1980s. The President's Council on Physical Fitness and Sports was one result of the Kraus-Weber test results.

28. **In 1956, the AAHPER Fitness Conferences established: (Rigorous) (Skill 2.1)**
   A. The President's Council on Youth Fitness
   B. The President's Citizens' Advisory Committee
   C. The President's Council on Physical Fitness
   D. A and B

(D., A., and B.) The **President's Council on Youth Fitness** was founded on July 16, 1956 to encourage American children to be healthy and active after a study indicated that American youths were less physically fit than European children. President Eisenhower created the President's Council on Youth Fitness with cabinet-level status. The Executive Order specified "one" objective. The first Council identified itself as a "catalytic agent" concentrating on creating public awareness. A President's Citizens-Advisory Committee on Fitness of American Youth was confirmed to give advice to the Council.

29. **Students that paddle balls against a wall or jump over objects with various heights are demonstrating which quality of movement? (Rigorous) (Skill 2.1)**
   A. Balance
   B. Time
   C. Force
   D. Inertia

(C.) Force is the capacity to do work or create physical change, energy, strength, or active power. It is a classical **force** that causes a free body with mass to accelerate. A net (or resultant) force that causes such acceleration may be the non-zero additive sum of many different forces acting on a body.

PHYSICAL EDUCATION

TEACHER CERTIFICATION STUDY GUIDE

30. **All of the following affect force except: (Easy) (Skill 2.1)**
    A. Magnitude
    B. Energy
    C. Motion
    D. Mass

(D.) Mass is a property of a physical object that quantifies the amount of matter and energy it contains. Unlike weight, the mass of something stays the same regardless of location. Every object has a unified body of matter with no specific shape.

31. **For a movement to occur, applied force must overcome inertia of an object and any other resisting forces. What concept of force does this describe? (Rigorous) (Skill 2.1)**
    A. Potential energy
    B. Magnitude
    C. Kinetic energy
    D. Absorption

(B.) Speaking of magnitude in a purely relative way states that nothing is large and nothing small. If everything in the universe were increased in bulk one thousand diameters, nothing would be any larger than it was before. However, if one thing remained unchanged, all of the others would be larger than they had been. To a person familiar with the relativity of magnitude and distance, the spaces and masses of the astronomer would be no more impressive than those of the microscopist. To the contrary, the visible universe may be a small part of an atom, with its component ions floating in the life-fluid (luminiferous ether) of some animal.

32. **The energy of an object to do work while recoiling is which type of potential energy? (Average Rigor) (Skill 2.1)**
    A. Absorption
    B. Kinetic
    C. Elastic
    D. Torque

(C.) In materials science, the word elastomer refers to a material that is very elastic (like rubber). The word elastic is often used colloquially to refer to an elastomeric material such as rubber or cloth/rubber combinations. It is capable of withstanding stress without injury. Elastic potential energy describes the energy inherent in flexible objects.

33. **Gradually decelerating a moving mass by utilization of smaller forces over a long period of time is: (Average Rigor) (Skill 2.1)**
    A. Stability
    B. Equilibrium
    C. Angular force
    D. Force absorption

(D.) Force absorption is the gradual deceleration of a moving mass by utilization of smaller forces over a long period of time.

34. **Which of the following principles is not a factor to assess or correct errors in performance for process assessment? (Average Rigor) (Skill 2.1)**
    A. Inertia
    B. Action/Reaction
    C. Force
    D. Acceleration

(C.) Force is not a factor to focus on in process assessment.

35. **An instructor used a similar movement from a skill learned in a different activity to teach a skill for a new activity. The technique used to facilitate cognitive learning was: (Rigorous) (Skill 2.1)**
    A. Conceptual thinking
    B. Transfer of learning
    C. Longer instruction
    D. Appropriate language

(B.) Using a previously used movement to facilitate a new task is a transfer of learning. The individual relates the past activity to the new one, enabling him/her to learn it more easily. Conceptual thinking is related to the transfer of learning, but it does not give the exact idea. Rather, it emphasizes the history of all learning.

36. **A teacher rewards students for completing tasks. Which method is the teacher using to facilitate psychomotor learning? (Average Rigor) (Skill 2.1)**
    A. Task/Reciprocal
    B. Command/Direct
    C. Contingency/Contract
    D. Physical/Reflex

(C.) Since the teacher is rewarding the student, the contingency/contract method is in place. The command/direct method involves the interaction between student and teacher when the student fails to fulfill the requirements.

37. The Round Hill School (a private school) in Massachusetts was the first school to require P.E. in its curriculum. What year was this? (Average Rigor) (Skill 2.1)
    A. 1792
    B. 1823
    C. 1902
    D. 1806

(B.) Requiring physical education in its curriculum in 1823, The Round Hill School paved the wave for public schools to follow suit, beginning in 1866 in California.

38. All of the following are Systematic Observational Evaluations except: (Rigorous) (Skill 2.3)
    A. Reflective Recording
    B. Event Recording
    C. Duration Recording
    D. Self Recording

(A.) Reflective recording is not a type of systematic observational evaluation. Event, duration, and self recordings are all methods used in systematic observational evaluations.

39. What year did California enact a law requiring all public schools to include physical education in its curriculum: (Easy) (Skill 2.1)
    A. 1892
    B. 1866
    C. 1901
    D. 1899

(B.) In 1866 the California legislature became the first state public school system to require physical education in their schools curriculums.

40. Title IX ensured that: (Easy) (Skill 3.1)
    A. Boys play baseball while girls play softball
    B. Girls are ensured the same educational and athletic opportunities as boys
    C. Girls and boys have coed physical education classes
    D. All students must dress out for physical education class

(B.) In 1972, Title IX was passed that ensured the same educational and athletic opportunities for both girls and boys. If a male sport was offered, then the same or a similar sport had to be offered for girls, otherwise the girls were allowed to try out for the boys sport team.

41. Through physical activities, John has developed self-discipline, fairness, respect for others, and new friends. John has demonstrated which of the following? (Rigorous) (Skill 3.1)
    A. Positive cooperation psycho-social influences
    B. Positive group psycho-social influences
    C. Positive individual psycho-social influences
    D. Positive accomplishment psycho-social influences

(B.) Through physical activities, John developed his social interaction skills. Social interaction is the sequence of social actions between individuals (or groups) that modify their actions and reactions due to the actions of their interaction partner(s). In other words, they are events in which people attach meaning to a situation, interpret what others mean, and respond accordingly. Through socialization with other people, John feels the influence of the people around him.

42. Which of the following psycho-social influences is not considered negative? (Rigorous) (Skill 3.1)
    A. Avoidance of problems
    B. Adherence to exercise
    C. Ego-centeredness
    D. Role conflict

(B.) The ability of an individual to adhere to an exercise routine due to her/his excitement, accolades, etc. is not considered a negative psycho-social influence. Adherence to an exercise routine is healthy and positive.

43. The affective domain of physical education contributes to all of the following except: (Rigorous) (Skill 3.1)
    A. Knowledge of exercise, health, and disease
    B. Self-actualization
    C. An appreciation of beauty
    D. Good sportsmanship

(A.) The affective domain encompasses emotions, thoughts, and feelings related to physical education. Knowledge of exercise, health, and disease is part of the cognitive domain.

TEACHER CERTIFICATION STUDY GUIDE

44. **A physical education instructor anticipates and prevents potential injuries, watches for hidden injuries, and takes an injury evaluation of the entire class. Which of the following strategies to prevent injuries is the teacher demonstrating? (Average Rigor) (Skill 3.1)**
    A. Maintaining hiring standards
    B. Proper use of equipment
    C. Proper procedures for emergencies
    D. Participant screening

(D.) In order for the instructor to know each student's physical status, she takes an injury evaluation. Such surveys are one way to know the physical status of an individual. It chronicles past injuries, tattoos, activities, and diseases the individual may have or had. It helps the instructor to know the limitations of each individual. Participant screening covers all forms of surveying and anticipation of injuries.

45. **An instructor notices that class participation is much lower than expected. By making changes in equipment and rules, the instructor applied which of the following concepts to enhance participation? (Rigorous) (Skill 3.1)**
    A. Homogeneous grouping
    B. Heterogeneous grouping
    C. Multi-activity designs
    D. Activity modification

(D.) Activity modification involves changing rules and equipment to fit the needs of students of different ability levels and physical development levels. Activity modification can encourage participation by making games and activities more enjoyable and allowing more student success.

46. **Using tactile clues is a functional adaptation that can assist which type of students? (Rigorous) (Skill 3.1)**
    A. Deaf students
    B. Blind students
    C. Asthmatic students
    D. Physically challenged students

(B.) Blind people use tactile clues to identify colors. Instructors should use tactile clues to help students see or hear targets by adding color, making them larger, or moving them closer. It will help cooperation in a creative way.

PHYSICAL EDUCATION

TEACHER CERTIFICATION STUDY GUIDE

47. There are two sequential phases to the development of spatial awareness. What is the order of these phases? (Rigorous) (Skill 3.1)
   A. Locating more than one object to each object; the location of objects in relation to one's own body in space.
   B. The location of objects in relation to ones' own body in space; locating more than one object in relation to one's own body.
   C. Locating more than one object independent of one's body; the location of objects in relation to one's own body.
   D. The location of objects in relation to one's own body in space; locating more than one object in relation to each object and independent of one's own body.

(D.) The order of the two sequential phases to develop spatial awareness are as follows: the location of objects in relation to one's own body in space, and locating more than one object in relation to each object and independent of one's own body.

48. Equilibrium is maintained as long as: (Average Rigor) (Skill 3.1)
   A. Body segments are moved independently.
   B. The center of gravity is over the base of support
   C. Force is applied to the base of support.
   D. The center of gravity is lowered.

(B.) Equilibrium is a condition in which all acting influences are canceled by others, resulting in a stable, balanced, or unchanging system. It allows humans and animals to walk without falling. An object maintains equilibrium as long as its center of gravity is over its base of support.

49. Which of the following does not enhance equilibrium? (Average Rigor) (Skill 3.1)
   A. Shifting the center of gravity away from the direction of movement.
   B. Increasing the base of support.
   C. Lowering the base of support.
   D. Increasing the base of support and lowering the center of support.

(A.) Equilibrium is a state of balance. When a body or a system is in equilibrium, there is no net tendency toward change. In mechanics, equilibrium has to do with the forces acting on a body. When no force acts to make a body move in a line, the body is in translational equilibrium. When no force acts to make the body turn, the body is in rotational equilibrium. A body in equilibrium while at rest is said to be in static equilibrium. Increasing the base of support, lowering the base of support, and increasing the base of support and lowering the center of support all enhance equilibrium by balancing forces.

PHYSICAL EDUCATION

TEACHER CERTIFICATION STUDY GUIDE

50. **The most effective way to promote the physical education curriculum is to: (Rigorous) (Skill 3.2)**
    A. Relate physical education to higher thought processes
    B. Relate physical education to humanitarianism
    C. Relate physical education to the total educational process
    D. Relate physical education to skills necessary to preserve the natural environment

(C.) The government treats the physical education curriculum as one of the major subjects. Because of all the games that we now participate in, many countries have focused their hearts and set their minds on competing with rival countries. Physical education is now one of the major, important subjects and instructors should integrate physical education into the total educational process.

51. **Which of the following is not a consideration for the selection of a facility? (Rigorous) (Skill 3.2)**
    A. Community involvement
    B. Custodial staff
    C. Availability to women, minorities, and the handicapped
    D. Bond issues

(A.) While community involvement positively impacts the communities where individuals live and work, it is not a major consideration in facility selection. Factors that are more important are staffing, accessibility, and financial considerations.

52. **Which of the following is not a class-management technique? (Easy) (Skill 3.2)**
    A. Explaining procedures for roll call, excuses, and tardiness
    B. Explaining routines for changing and showering
    C. Explaining conditioning
    D. Promoting individual self-discipline

(C.) Explaining conditioning is not a class management technique. It is an instructional lesson.

53. **Long-term planning is essential for effective class management. Identify the management techniques not essential to long-term planning. (Easy) (Skill 3.2)**
    A. Parental observation
    B. Progress evaluation
    C. Precise activity planning
    D. Arrangements for line markings

(A.) While it is important that a child have support from his/her parents, parental observation is not an essential consideration in long-term planning. Progress evaluation, precise activity planning, and arranging line markings are all essential management techniques for long-term planning.

PHYSICAL EDUCATION

TEACHER CERTIFICATION STUDY GUIDE

54. **Although Mary is a paraplegic, she wants to participate in some capacity in the physical education class. What federal legislative act entitles her to do so? (Rigorous) (Skill 3.2)**
    A. PE 94-142
    B. Title IX
    C. PL 94-142
    D. Title XI

(C.) It is the purpose of Act PL 94-142 to assure that all handicapped children have available to them, within the time periods specified in section 612(2), (B.), a free, appropriate public education that emphasizes special education and related services designed to meet their unique needs, to assure that the rights of handicapped children and their parents/guardians are protected, to assist states and localities to provide for the education of all handicapped children, and to assess and assure the effectiveness of efforts to educate handicapped children.

55. **A legal wrong resulting in a direct or an indirect injury is: (Average Rigor) (Skill 3.2)**
    A. Negligence
    B. A Tort
    C. In loco parentis
    D. Legal liability

(B.) A tort is damage, injury, or a wrongful act done willfully, negligently, or in circumstances involving strict liability, but not involving breach of contract, for which a civil suit can be brought.

56. **All of the following actions help avoid lawsuits except: (Average Rigor) (Skill 3.2)**
    A. Ensuring equipment and facilities are safe
    B. Getting exculpatory agreements
    C. Knowing each students' health status
    D. Grouping students with unequal competitive levels

(D.) Grouping students with unequal competitive levels is not an action that can help avoid lawsuits. Such a practice could lead to injury because of the inequality in skill, size, and strength.

57. **Which of the following actions does not promote safety? (Rigorous) (Skill 3.2)**
    A. Allowing students to wear the current style of shoes
    B. Presenting organized activities
    C. Inspecting equipment and facilities
    D. Instructing skill and activities properly

(A.) Shoes are very important in physical education and the emphasis on current shoe styles does not promote safety because they focus more on the look of the clothing, rather than functionality.

58. The tendency of a body/object to remain in its present state of motion unless some force acts to change it is which mechanical principle of motion? (Average Rigor) (Skill 3.2)
   A. Acceleration
   B. Inertia
   C. Action/Reaction
   D. Linear motion

(B.) Inertia (ĭnûr'shə) is a term used in physics that describes the resistance of a body to any alteration in its state of motion. Inertia is a property common to all matter. This property was first observed by Galileo and was later restated by Newton. Newton's first law of motion is sometimes called the law of inertia. Newton's second law of motion states that the external force required to affect the motion of a body is proportional to the acceleration. The constant of proportionality is known as the mass, which is the numerical value of the inertia. The greater the inertia of a body, the less acceleration is needed for a given, applied force.

59. The movement response of a system depends not only on the net external force, but also on the resistance to movement change. Which mechanical principle of motion does this definition describe? (Rigorous) (Skill 3.2)
   A. Acceleration
   B. Inertia
   C. Action/Reaction
   D. Air Resistance

(A.) Acceleration is the change in the velocity of a body with respect to time. Since velocity is a vector quantity involving both magnitude and direction, acceleration is also a vector. In order to produce acceleration, a force must act on a body. The magnitude of the force (F) must be directly proportional to both the mass of the body (m) and the desired acceleration (a), according to Newton's second law of motion ($F=ma$). The exact nature of the acceleration depends on the relative directions of the original velocity and force. A force acting in the same direction as the velocity changes only the speed of the body. An appropriate force, acting always at right angles to the velocity, changes the direction of the velocity but not the speed.

60. **Which of the following mechanical principles of motion states that every motion has a similar, contrasting response? (Easy) (Skill 3.2)**
    A. Acceleration
    B. Inertia
    C. Action/Reaction
    D. Centripetal force

(C.) The principle of action/reaction is an assertion about the nature of motion from which we can determine the trajectory of an object subject to forces. The path of an object yields a stationary value for a quantity called the **action**. Thus, instead of thinking about an object accelerating in response to applied forces, one might think of them as picking out the path with a stationary action.

61. **A subjective, observational approach to identify errors in the form, style, or mechanics of a skill is accomplished by: (Rigorous) (Skill 4.1)**
    A. Product assessment
    B. Process assessment
    C. Standardized norm-referenced tests
    D. Criterion-referenced tests

(B.) Process assessment is one way to identify errors in the skills of an individual. It is one way to know the limitations and skills that every individual possesses.

62. **What type of assessment objectively measures skill performance? (Rigorous) (Skill 4.1)**
    A. Process assessment
    B. Product assessment
    C. Texas PE Test
    D. Iowa Brace Test

(B.) Product assessment measures the skills of an individual. This process is a methodical evaluation of the characteristics of your product or service in the eyes of potential users and customers. The two principle types of assessments are principle-based assessments and usability testing.

63. **Process assessment does not identify which of the following errors in skill performance? (Average Rigor) (Skill 4.1)**
    A. Style
    B. Form
    C. End result
    D. Mechanics

(C.) Process assessment does not evaluate end results. Process assessment emphasizes analysis of style, form, and mechanics.

TEACHER CERTIFICATION STUDY GUIDE

64. **Determining poor performance of a skill using process assessment can best be accomplished by: (Average Rigor) (Skill 4.1)**
    A. Observing how fast a skill is performed.
    B. Observing how many skills are performed.
    C. Observing how far or how high a skill is performed.
    D. Observing several attributes comprising the entire performance of a skill.

(D.) To determine the source of the error in the poor performance of an individual, we use observations of several attributes that compromise the entire performance of a skill. Instructors should observe limitations and mistakes and determine how to best address these problems to improve future performance.

65. **Which of the following methods measures fundamental skills using product assessment? (Rigorous) (Skill 4.1)**
    A. Criterion-referenced tests
    B. Standardized norm-referenced tests
    C. Both A and B
    D. Neither A nor B

(C.) Criterion-referenced tests and standardized norm-referenced tests are both methods that can prove and measure skills in product assessment. They can help to prevent or lessen errors.

66. **Product assessment measures all of the following except: (Rigorous) (Skill 4.1)**
    A. How the student performs the mechanics of a skill.
    B. How many times the student performs a skill.
    C. How fast the student performs a skill.
    D. How far or high the student performs a skill.

(A.) Product assessment evaluates student performance and gives insight into how students can correct errors. Product assessment measures results. Thus, how the student performs the mechanics of a skill is not relevant to product assessment.

67. **Instructors can evaluate skill level of achievement in archery by: (Average Rigor) (Skill 4.1)**
    A. Giving students a written exam on terminology.
    B. Having students demonstrate the correct tension of arrow feathers.
    C. Totaling a student's score obtained on the target's face.
    D. Time how long a student takes to shoot all arrows.

(C.) Archery is the practice of using a bow to shoot arrows. Totaling a student's score is the only method, of the possible choices, that evaluates skill level. Choices A and B test knowledge and choice D is an arbitrary measure.

TEACHER CERTIFICATION STUDY GUIDE

68. **Instructors can determine skill level achievement in golf by: (Average Rigor) (Skill 4.1)**
    A. The number of "birdies" that were made.
    B. The number of "bogies" that were made.
    C. The score obtained after several rounds.
    D. The total score achieved throughout the school year.

(C.) Instructors can determine skill level in golf by evaluating a golfer's score after several rounds. The number of bogies or birdies is not necessarily indicative of skill level because they are isolated events (i.e. the score on one hole). The player who consistently scores the lowest likely has the most impressive golf skills. Therefore, a player's score is the best way to determine his/her skill level. Finally, several rounds are a sufficient sample to determine skill level. An entire year's worth of scores is not necessary.

69. **Instructors can determine skill level achievement in swimming by: (Average Rigor) (Skill 4.1)**
    A. How long a student can float.
    B. How many strokes it takes to swim a specified distance.
    C. How long a student can stay under the water without moving.
    D. How many times a student can dive in five minutes.

(B.) Instructors can determine skill level in swimming by counting the strokes a swimmer takes when covering a certain distance. The arm movement, the strength, and the tactic to move quickly give the swimmer an ability to swim faster. The ability to float, stay under water, and dive quickly is not relevant to swimming ability.

70. **Instructors can assess skill level achievement in bowling by: (Easy) (Skill 4.1)**
    A. Calculating a student's average.
    B. Calculating how many gutter-balls were thrown.
    C. Calculating how many strikes were thrown.
    D. Calculating how many spares were thrown.

(A.) Instructors can determine the skill level of a bowler by calculating the student's average game score. There is a possibility that some coincidences take place (e.g., bowling a strike). To check the consistency, we determine the average instead of looking at only the score from a single game.

PHYSICAL EDUCATION

71. Although they are still hitting the target, the score of some students practicing archery has decreased as the distance between them and the target has increased. Which of the following adjustments will improve their scores? (Rigorous) (Skill 4.1)
    A. Increasing the velocity of their arrows.
    B. Increasing the students' base of support.
    C. Increasing the weight of the arrows.
    D. Increasing the parabolic path of the arrows.

(D.) Increasing the parabolic path of the arrows will increase accuracy and precision at greater distances.

72. Some students practicing basketball are having difficulty with "free throws," even though the shots make it to and over the hoop. What adjustment will improve their "free throws"? (Average Rigor) (Skill 4.1)
    A. Increasing the height of release (i.e. jump shot).
    B. Increasing the vertical path of the ball.
    C. Increasing the velocity of the release.
    D. Increasing the base of support.

(B.) In this case, increasing the vertical path of the ball will help the students make more free throws. Increased vertical path provides greater margin for error, allowing the ball to drop more easily through the hoop. Increasing the velocity cannot work due to common sense. Finally, increasing the height of release and base of support are not viable options in this case because the students are having no problem getting the ball to the basket.

73. An archery student's arrow bounced off the red part of the target face. What is the correct ruling? (Average Rigor) (Skill 4.1)
    A. No score.
    B. Re-shoot arrow.
    C. 7 points awarded.
    D. Shot receives same score as highest arrow shot that did not bounce off the target.

(C.) When an arrow bounces off the red area of a target, the archer receives 7 points; the value of the shot had the arrow stuck in the target.

74. A student playing badminton believed that the shuttlecock was going to land out-of-bounds. The shuttlecock landed on the line. What is the correct ruling? (Easy) (Skill 4.1)
    A. The shuttlecock is out-of-bounds.
    B. The shuttlecock is in-bounds.
    C. The point is replayed.
    D. That player is charged with a feint.

(B.) If a shuttlecock lands on the line, it is inbounds by the rules of badminton.

75. **A mechanical pinsetter accidentally knocked down the only bowling pin left standing for a spare attempt, after clearing all the other pins knocked down by the first ball thrown. What is the correct ruling? (Rigorous) (Skill 4.1)**
    A. Foul
    B. Spare
    C. Frame is replayed
    D. No count for that pin

(D.) When the mechanical pin setter touches a pin and knocks it down, there is no count for the pin because the pin fell because of mechanical fault and the player had nothing to do with it. The other pins count and there is no foul for the player.

76. **The ball served in racquetball hits the front line and lands in front of the short line. What is the ruling? (Easy) (Skill 4.1)**
    A. Fault
    B. Reserve
    C. Out-of-bounds
    D. Fair ball

(A.) If a served ball falls in front of the short line, it is a fault according to a rule that states that a ball must fall within the short line frame at the time of serving. It is not out-of-bounds, as it is still within the limits of the pitch. However, it is also not a fair ball due to the service rule.

77. **Two opposing soccer players are trying to gain control of the ball when one player "knees" the other. What is the ruling? (Easy) (Skill 4.1)**
    A. Direct free kick
    B. Indirect free kick
    C. Fair play
    D. Ejection from a game

(A.) Assuming that the soccer player didn't intentionally hit the other player's knee, the result would be a direct free kick. If the foul was intentional, the referee can eject the offender from the game. Minor offenses and offenses not involving contact result in indirect free kicks.

TEACHER CERTIFICATION STUDY GUIDE

78. **Two students are playing badminton. When receiving the shuttlecock, one student consistently stands too deep in the receiving court. What strategy should the server use to serve the shuttlecock? (Average Rigor) (Skill 4.1)**
    A. Smash serve
    B. Clear serve
    C. Overhead serve
    D. Short serve

(D.) The short serve would land short in the court so the opponent would not be able to reach the shuttlecock. Therefore, the short serve would win the point. A clear or overhead serve enables the opponent to hit the shuttlecock and continue the game. A smash serve runs a higher risk of falling out-of-bounds. Neither of these scenarios are goals of the server.

79. **A basketball team has an outstanding rebounder. In order to keep this player near the opponent's basket, which strategy should the coach implement? (Easy) (Skill 4.1)**
    A. Pick-and-Roll
    B. Give-and-Go
    C. Zone defense
    D. Free-lancing

(C.) A zone defense, where each player guards an area of the court rather than an individual player, allows an outstanding rebounder to remain near the basket. The give-and-go, pick-and-roll, and free-lancing are offensive strategies that do not affect rebounding.

80. **When a defensive tennis player needs more time to return to his position, what strategy should he apply? (Rigorous) (Skill 4.1)**
    A. Drop shot
    B. Dink shot
    C. Lob shot
    D. Down-the-line shot

(C.) When a tennis player is off the court and needs time to return to his position, the player should play a lob shot. Down-the-line shots and drop shots are offensive shots and are too risky in this situation. The dink shot would allow the opponent to take control of the point.

81. **An overhead badminton stroke used to hit a forehand-like overhead stroke that is on the backhand side of the body is called:** (Rigorous) (Skill 4.1)
    A. Around-the-head-shot
    B. Down-the-line shot
    C. Lifting the shuttle
    D. Under hand shuttle

(A.) A shot played from the backhand side and over the head is known as an around-the-head shot. It is played when the shuttlecock is high and cannot be reached any other way.

82. **A maneuver when an offensive player passes to a teammate and then immediately cuts in toward the basket for a return pass is:** (Average Rigor) (Skill 4.1)
    A. Charging
    B. Pick
    C. Give-and-go
    D. Switching

(C.) In the game of basketball, a give-and-go is an offensive play where a player passes to a teammate and immediately cuts towards the basket for a return pass. Charging is an offensive foul, a pick is a maneuver to free up a teammate for a pass or shot, and switching is a defensive maneuver.

83. **A bowling pin that remains standing after an apparently perfect hit is called a:** (Rigorous) (Skill 4.1)
    A. Tap
    B. Turkey
    C. Blow
    D. Leave

(A.) A bowling pin that remains standing, even after a perfect shot, is known as a tap. Other options, like turkeys and blows, are not relevant to the standing pin.

84. **A soccer pass from the outside of the field near the end line to a position in front of the goal is called:** (Average Rigor) (Skill 4.1)
    A. Chip
    B. Settle
    C. Through
    D. Cross

(D.) Any long pass from the sides of the field toward the middle is a cross, since the hitter hits it across the field. A chip is a high touch pass or shot. A through pass travels the length of the field through many players. Finally, settling is the act of controlling the ball after receiving a pass.

TEACHER CERTIFICATION STUDY GUIDE

85. A volleyball that is simultaneously contacted above the net by opponents and momentarily held upon contact is called a/an: (Easy) (Skill 4.1)
    A. Double fault
    B. Play over
    C. Overlap
    D. Held ball

(D.) In volleyball, if two players simultaneously contact the ball above the net, the ball is a held ball.

86. Volleyball player LB on team A digs a spiked ball. The ball deflects off LB's shoulder. What is the ruling? (Average Rigor) (Skill 4.1)
    A. Fault
    B. Legal hit
    C. Double foul
    D. Play over

(B.) Since the spiked ball does not touch the ground and instead deflects off LB's shoulder, it is a legal hit. In order for a point to end, the ball must touch the ground. In this instance, it does not.

87. Playing "Simon Says" and having students touch different body parts applies which movement concept? (Average Rigor) (Skill 4.2)
    A. Spatial Awareness
    B. Effort Awareness
    C. Body Awareness
    D. Motion Awareness

(C.) Body Awareness is a method that integrates European traditions of movement and biomedical knowledge with the East Asian traditions of movement (e.g. Tai chi and Zen meditation).

88. Having students move in a specific pattern while measuring how long they take to do so develops which quality of movement? (Average Rigor) (Skill 4.2)
    A. Balance
    B. Time
    C. Force
    D. Inertia

(B.) Time is a sequential arrangement of all events or the interval between two events in such a sequence. We can discuss the concept of time on several different levels: physical, psychological, philosophical, scientific, and biological. Time is the non-spatial continuum in which events occur, in apparently irreversible succession, from the past through the present to the future.

89. Aerobic dance develops or improves each of the following skills or health components except... (Rigorous) (Skill 4.2)
    A. Cardio-respiratory function
    B. Body composition
    C. Coordination
    D. Flexibility

(D.) Aerobic dance does not develop flexibility, as flexibility results from stretching and not aerobic exercise. Ballet dancing, however, does develop flexibility. Aerobic dance develops cardio-respiratory function due to the unusual body movements performed. It also improves body composition and coordination due to the movement of various body parts.

90. Rowing develops which health or skill related component of fitness?
    A. Muscle endurance (Rigorous) (Skill 4.2)
    B. Flexibility
    C. Balance
    D. Reaction time

(A.) Rowing helps develop muscle endurance because of the continuous arm movement against the force of the water. Flexibility, balance, and reaction time are not important components of rowing. Rowing also develops the lower abdominal muscles while the individual is in the sitting position when rowing.

91. Calisthenics develops all of the following health and skill related components of fitness except: (Average Rigor) (Skill 4.2)
    A. Muscle strength
    B. Body composition
    C. Power
    D. Agility

(C.) Calisthenics is a sport that actually helps to keep a body fit in by combining gymnastic and aerobic activities. Calisthenics develop muscle strength and agility and improves body composition. However, calisthenics does not develop power because they do not involve resistance training or explosiveness.

92. Which health or skill related component of fitness is developed by rope jumping? (Average Rigor) (Skill 4.2)
    A. Muscle Force
    B. Coordination
    C. Flexibility
    D. Muscle strength

(B.) Rope jumping is a good mental exercise and it improves coordination. Many athletes (e.g. boxers, tennis players) jump rope to improve coordination and quickness. Muscle strength is secondary to that.

93. Swimming does not improve which health or skill related component of fitness? (Rigorous) (Skill 4.2)
    A. Cardio-respiratory function
    B. Flexibility
    C. Muscle strength
    D. Foot Speed

(D.) Swimming involves every part of the body. It works on the cardio-respiratory system and it develops flexibility because of the intense body movement in the water. It also improves muscle strength as swimmers must move their bodies against the force of water. Increased foot speed is not an outcome of swimming.

94. Data from a cardio-respiratory assessment can identify and predict all of the following except: (Rigorous) (Skill 4.2)
    A. Functional aerobic capacity
    B. Natural over-fatness
    C. Running ability
    D. Motivation

(B.) The data from cardio-respiratory assessment can identify and predict running ability, motivation, and functional aerobic capacity. However, it cannot predict natural over-fatness, as natural over-fatness is a part of the human body. It is not artificially developed like running ability and motivation.

95. Data from assessing _____ identifies an individual's potential of developing musculoskeletal problems and an individual's potential of performing activities of daily living. (Rigorous) (Skill 4.2)
    A. Flexibility
    B. Muscle endurance
    C. Muscle strength
    D. Motor performance

(A.) Flexibility.

96. **A 17-year-old male student performed 20 sit-ups, ran a mile in 8 minutes, and has a body fat composition of 17%. Which is the best interpretation of his fitness level? (Rigorous) (Skill 4.2)**
    A. Average muscular endurance, good cardiovascular endurance; appropriate body fat composition.
    B. Low muscular endurance, average cardiovascular endurance; high body fat composition.
    C. Low muscular endurance, average cardiovascular endurance; appropriate body fat composition.
    D. Low muscular endurance, low cardiovascular endurance; appropriate body fat composition.

(**C.**) A 17-year-old male who performs 20 sit-ups, runs a mile in 8 minutes and has 17% fat composition has low muscular endurance, average cardiovascular endurance, and appropriate fat composition. 20 sit-ups is a relatively low number. An 8-minute mile is an average time for a 17-year-old male. Finally, a body fat composition of 17% is appropriate.

97. **Based on the information given in the previous question, what changes would you recommend to improve this person's level of fitness? (Average Rigor) (Skill 4.2)**
    A. Muscle endurance training and cardiovascular endurance training.
    B. Muscle endurance training, cardiovascular endurance training, and reduction of caloric intake.
    C. Muscle strength training and cardio-vascular endurance training.
    D. No changes necessary.

(**A.**) The person requires both muscle endurance and cardiovascular training while keeping the other bodily intakes normal. An appropriate program would include moderate weightlifting and regular aerobic activity.

98. **An obese student's fitness assessments were poor for every component of fitness. Which would you recommend first? (Easy) (Skill 4.2)**
    A. A jogging program.
    B. A weight lifting program.
    C. A walking program.
    D. A stretching program.

(**C.**) An obese person should begin by walking and then progress to jogging. Weightlifting and stretching are not as important initially. They are also dangerous because the student may not have the ability to complete such strenuous tasks safely.

TEACHER CERTIFICATION STUDY GUIDE

99. Coordinated movements that project a person over an obstacle are known as: (Easy) (Skill 4.4)
    A. Jumping
    B. Vaulting
    C. Leaping
    D. Hopping

(B.) Vaulting is the art of acrobatics on horseback. Vaulting is an internationally recognized, competitive sport that is growing in popularity. At the most basic level vaulting enhances riding skills. At any skill-level, this ancient dance between horse and rider deepens the sense of balance, timing, and poise for the rider, as well as a sensitivity to and respect for the horse-rider relationship. Vaulting in competition can be done individually or on a team of 8 people with up to 3 people on the horse at once.

100. Which manipulative skill uses the hands to stop the momentum of an object? (Rigorous) (Skill 4.4)
    A. Trapping
    B. Catching
    C. Striking
    D. Rolling

(B.) The ability to use the hands to catch an object is a manipulative skill. Catching stops the momentum of an object. A successful catch harnesses the force of the oncoming object to stop the object's momentum.

101. Which professional organization protects amateur sports from corruption? (Easy) (Skill 5.1)
    A. AIWA
    B. AAHPERD
    C. NCAA
    D. AAU

(D.) The Amateur Athletic Union (AAU) is one of the largest non-profit, volunteer sports organizations in the United States. A multi-sport organization, the AAU dedicates itself exclusively to the promotion and development of amateur sports and physical fitness programs. Answer C may be a tempting choice, but the NCAA deals only with college athletics.

102. Which professional organization works with legislatures? (Average Rigor) (Skill 5.1)
    A. AIWA
    B. AAHPERD
    C. ACSM
    D. AAU

(B.) AAHPERD, or American Alliance for Health, Physical Education, Recreation and Dance, is an alliance of 6 national associations. AAHPERD is the largest organization of professionals supporting and assisting those involved in physical education, leisure, fitness, dance, health promotion, and education, as well as all other specialties related to achieving a healthy lifestyle. AAHPERD is an alliance designed to provide members with a comprehensive and coordinated array of resources, support, and programs to help practitioners improve their skills and in turn, further the health and well-being of the American public.

103. Research in physical education is published in all of the following periodicals except the: (Average Rigor) (Skill 5.1)
    A. School PE Update
    B. Research Quarterly
    C. Journal of Physical Education
    D. YMCA Magazine

(A.) Each school has a PE Update that publishes their own periodicals about physical activities. It aims at helping the students to catch-up on what is happening around them. The school produces this update to encourage their students to become more interested in all of the physical activities that they offer. School PE Updates, however, do not include research findings.

104. A teacher who modifies and develops tasks for a class is demonstrating knowledge of which appropriate behavior in physical education activities? (Rigorous) (Skill 5.1)
    A. Appropriate management behavior
    B. Appropriate student behavior
    C. Appropriate administration behavior
    D. Appropriate content behavior

(D.) In this case, the teacher is demonstrating knowledge of a behavior in reference to physical activity. It is known as appropriate content behavior. The other options are not related to physical activities.

105. **The ability for a muscle(s) to repeatedly contract over a period of time is: (Average Rigor) (Skill 5.1)**
    A. Cardiovascular endurance
    B. Muscle endurance
    C. Muscle strength
    D. Muscle force

(B.) Muscle endurance gives the muscle the ability to contract over a period of time. Muscle strength is a prerequisite for the endurance of muscle. Cardiovascular endurance involves aerobic exercise.

106. **The ability to change rapidly the direction of the body is: (Average Rigor) (Skill 5.1)**
    A. Coordination
    B. Reaction time
    C. Speed
    D. Agility

(D.) Agility is the ability of the body to change position quickly. Reaction time, coordination, and speed are not the right words to describe the ability to move quickly, as we always say that the goalkeeper is agile.

107. **Students are performing the vertical jump. What component of fitness does this activity assess? (Rigorous) (Skill 5.1)**
    A. Muscle strength
    B. Balance
    C. Power
    D. Muscle endurance

(C.) Vertical jumping assesses the power of the entire body. It shows the potential of the legs to hold the upper body and the strength in the joints of the legs. Balance and muscle strength are secondary requirements. Power automatically ensures these secondary requirements.

108. Using the Karvonen Formula, compute the 60% - 80% THR for a 16-year old student with a RHR of 60. (Rigorous) (Skill 5.1)
  A. 122-163 beats per minute
  B. 130-168 beats per minute
  C. 142-170 beats per minute
  D. 146-175 beats per minute

(D.) 220 – 16 (age) = 204, 204 – 60 (RHR) = 144, 144 x .60 (low end of heart range) = 86, 86 + 60 (RHR) = **146 (bottom of THR)**

220 – 16 (age) = 204, 204 – 60 (RHR) = 144, 144 x 0.80 (high end of heart range) = 115, 115 + (RHR) = **175 (top of THR)**

146-175 beats per minute is the 60%-80% THR.

109. Using Cooper's Formula, compute the THR for a 15-year old student. (Rigorous) (Skill 5.1)
  A. 120-153 beats per minute
  B. 123-164 beats per minute
  C. 135-169 beats per minute
  D. 147-176 beats per minute

(B.) 123-164 beats per minute.
THR = (200 – Age) x 0.6 to (220- Age) x 0.8 = (220 – 15) x 0.6 to (220- 15) x 0.8 = 123 to 164 beats per minute

110. Which is not a common negative stressor? (Rigorous) (Skill 5.1)
  A. Loss of significant other
  B. Personal illness or injury.
  C. Moving to a new state.
  D. Landing a new job.

(D.) Landing a new job is generally not a cause of worry or stress. In fact, it is a positive event. Personal illness, loss of a significant other, or moving to a strange state can cause negative stress.

TEACHER CERTIFICATION STUDY GUIDE

111. **Which of the following is a negative coping strategy for dealing with stress? (Average Rigor) (Skill 5.1)**
    A. Recreational diversions
    B. Active thinking
    C. Alcohol use
    D. Imagery

(C.) The use of alcohol is a negative coping strategy for dealing with stress. Alcohol causes the brain to lose the stressful data thus soothing the individual, but it can be highly detrimental in the long run. Positive ways to deal with stress include active thinking, imagery, and recreational diversions.

112. **The most important nutrient the body requires, without which life can only be sustained for a few days, is: (Easy) (Skill 5.1)**
    A. Vitamins
    B. Minerals
    C. Water
    D. Carbohydrates

(C.) Although the body requires vitamins, minerals, and carbohydrates to achieve proper growth and shape, water is essential. Without it, the body gets dehydrated and death is a possibility. Water should be pure, as seawater can cause kidney failure and death.

113. **With regard to protein content, foods from animal sources are usually: (Average Rigor) (Skill 5.1)**
    A. Complete
    B. Essential
    C. Nonessential
    D. Incidental

(A.) Animal protein is complete, meaning it provides all of the amino acids that the human body requires. Although animal meat is not essential to a person's diet, it is an excellent source of protein.

114. **Fats with room for two or more hydrogen atoms per molecule-fatty acid chain are: (Rigorous) (Skill 5.1)**
    A. Monounsaturated
    B. Polyunsaturated
    C. Hydrosaturated
    D. Saturated

(B.) Polyunsaturated fatty acids contain multiple carbon-carbon double bonds. Thus, there is room for two or more hydrogen atoms. Polyunsaturated fats are healthier than saturated fats.

PHYSICAL EDUCATION

115. **An adequate diet to meet nutritional needs consists of: (Rigorous) (Skill 5.1)**
    A. No more than 30% caloric intake from fats, no more than 50 % caloric intake from proteins, and at least 20% caloric intake from carbohydrates.
    B. No more than 30% caloric intake from fats, no more than 40% caloric intake from proteins, and at least 30% caloric intake from carbohydrates.
    C. No more than 30% caloric intake from fats, no more than 15% caloric intake from proteins, and at least 55% caloric intake from carbohydrates.
    D. No more than 30 % caloric intake from fats, no more than 30% caloric intake from proteins, and at least 40% caloric intake from carbohydrates.

(C.) General guidelines for nutritionally sound diets are 30% caloric intake from fats, no more than 15% caloric intake from proteins, and at least 55% caloric intake from carbohydrates.

116. **Maintaining body weight is best accomplished by: (Average Rigor) (Skill 5.1)**
    A. Dieting
    B. Aerobic exercise
    C. Lifting weights
    D. Equalizing caloric intake relative to output

(D.) The best way to maintain body weight is by balancing caloric intake and output. Extensive dieting (caloric restriction) is not a good option as this would result in weakness. Exercise is part of the output process that helps balance caloric input and output.

117. **Most high-protein diets: (Average Rigor) (Skill5.1)**
    A. Are high in cholesterol
    B. Are high in saturated fats
    C. Require vitamin and mineral supplements
    D. All of the above

(D.) High-protein diets are high in cholesterol, saturated fats, and they require vitamin and mineral supplements.

118. **Which one of the following statements about low-calorie diets is false? (Rigorous) (Skill 5.1)**
    A. Most people who "diet only" regain the weight they lose.
    B. They are the way most people try to lose weight.
    C. They make weight control easier.
    D. They lead to excess worry about weight, food, and eating.

(C.) People who participate in low-calorie diets do not control their weight easily. They must work more and utilize their bodies in many other ways (e.g., walking) to keep themselves fit.

119. **Physiological benefits of exercise include all of the following except: (Average Rigor) (Skill 5.1)**
    A. Reducing mental tension
    B. Improving muscle strength
    C. Cardiac hypertrophy
    D. Quicker recovery rate

(A.) Physical exercises can help improve muscle strength by making the body move and they can help provide quicker recovery between exercise sessions and from injuries. However, physical activity does not directly relieve mental tension. It might reduce tension temporarily, but chances are the tension will persist.

120. **Psychological benefits of exercise include all of the following except: (Rigorous) (Skill 5.1)**
    A. Improved sleeping patterns
    B. Improved energy regulation
    C. Improved appearance
    D. Improved quality of life

(B.) The psychological benefits of exercise include improved sleeping patterns, improved appearances, and an improved quality of life. Improved energy regulation is a physical benefit, not a psychological one.

121. **Which of the following conditions is not associated with a lack of physical activity? (Average Rigor) (Skill 5.1)**
    A. Atherosclerosis
    B. Longer life expectancy
    C. Osteoporosis
    D. Certain cancers

(B.) A lack of physical activity can contribute to atherosclerosis, osteoporosis, and certain cancers. Conversely, regular physical activity can contribute to longer life expectancy.

122. **Which of the following pieces of exercise equipment best applies the physiological principles? (Average Rigor) (Skill 5.1)**
    A. Rolling machine
    B. Electrical muscle stimulator
    C. Stationary Bicycle
    D. Motor-driven rowing machine

(C.) A stationary bicycle is the best option to support the body physically as it includes all of the operations related to an individual's body (e.g., movement of legs, position of arms, back exercise, stomach movement). Electrical muscle stimulators are very dangerous as they can cause muscles to loosen too much. Other machines may provide an unnecessarily extensive workout that is dangerous for muscles

TEACHER CERTIFICATION STUDY GUIDE

123. **To enhance skill and strategy performance for striking or throwing objects, for catching or collecting objects, and for carrying and propelling objects, students must first learn techniques for: (Rigorous) (Skill 5.3)**
    A. Offense
    B. Defense
    C. Controlling objects
    D. Continuous play of objects

(C.) For enhancing the catching, throwing, carrying, or propelling of objects, a student must learn how to control the objects. The control gives the player a sense of the object. Thus, offense, defense, and continuous play come naturally, as they are part of the controlling process.

124. **Which of the following is not a type of tournament? (Average Rigor) (Skill 5.3)**
    A. Spiderweb
    B. Pyramid
    C. Spiral
    D. Round Robin

(C.) A spiral is not a type of tournament.

125. **Which of the following is not a type of meet? (Average Rigor) (Skill 5.3)**
    A. Extramural
    B. Intramural
    C. Interscholastic
    D. Ladder

(D.) A ladder is not a type of meet.

126. **Activities to specifically develop cardiovascular fitness must be: (Rigorous) (Skill 6.1)**
    A. Performed without developing an oxygen debt
    B. Performed twice daily.
    C. Performed every day.
    D. Performed for a minimum of 10 minutes.

(A.) The development of cardiovascular fitness is not dependent on specific time limits or routine schedules. Participants should perform aerobic activities without developing an oxygen debt.

TEACHER CERTIFICATION STUDY GUIDE

127. **Which is not a sign of stress? (Average Rigor) (Skill 6.1)**
     A. Irritability
     B. Assertiveness
     C. Insomnia
     D. Stomach problems

(B.) Assertiveness is not a sign of stress. Irritability, insomnia, and stomach problems are all related to stress.

128. **Students are performing trunk extensions. What component of fitness does this activity assess? (Average Rigor) (Skill 9.1)**
     A. Balance
     B. Flexibility
     C. Body Composition
     D. Coordination

(B.) The core component of trunk extensions is flexibility. Trunk extension also indicates the body's capacity for full expansion and emphasizes areas such as the stomach, arms, and shoulder joints.

129. **Working at a level that is above normal is which exercise training principle? (Rigorous) (Skill 9.1)**
     A. Intensity
     B. Progression
     C. Specificity
     D. Overload

(D.) Overloading is exercising above normal capacities. Intensity and progression are supporting principles in the process of overload. Overloading can cause serious issues within the body, either immediately or after some time.

130. **Students on a running program to improve cardio-respiratory fitness apply which exercise principle? (Rigorous) (Skill 9.1)**
     A. Aerobic
     B. Progression
     C. Specificity
     D. Overload

(C.) Running to improve cardio-respiratory fitness is an example of specificity. Specificity is the selection of activities that isolate a specific body part or system. Aerobics is also a good option, but it deals with the entire body, including areas not specific to cardio-respiratory fitness.

TEACHER CERTIFICATION STUDY GUIDE

131. **Adding more reps to a weightlifting set applies which exercise principle? (Average Rigor) (Skill 9.1)**
    A. Anaerobic
    B. Progression
    C. Overload
    D. Specificity

(B.) Adding more repetitions (reps) to sets when weightlifting is an example of progression. Adding reps can result in overload, but the guiding principle is progression.

132. **Which of the following does not modify overload? (Rigorous) (Skill 9.1)**
    A. Frequency
    B. Perceived exertion
    C. Time
    D. Intensity

(B.) Time extension, frequency of movement, and intensity are all indicators of overload. However, exertion is not a good indicator of overload, because measuring exertion is subjective and difficult to monitor.

133. **Prior to activity, students perform a 5-10 minute warm-up. Which is not recommended as part of the warm-up? (Easy) (Skill 9.1)**
    A. Using the muscles that will be utilized in the following activity.
    B. Using a gradual aerobic warm-up.
    C. Using a gradual anaerobic warm-up.
    D. Stretching the major muscle groups to be used in the activity.

(C.) Warm-up is always necessary, but it should not be an anaerobic warm-up. The muscle exercises, the stretching, and even the aerobics are all helpful and athletes should complete these exercises within the normal breathing conditions. In fact, athletes should focus more closely on proper breathing. Athletes should engage in anaerobic stretching after activity, when muscles are loose and less prone to injury.

134. **Which is not a benefit of warming up? (Rigorous) (Skill 9.1)**
    A. Releasing hydrogen from myoglobin.
    B. Reducing the risk of musculoskeletal injuries.
    C. Raising the body's core temperature in preparation for activity.
    D. Stretching the major muscle groups to be used in the activity.

(A.) Warm-up can reduce the risk of musculoskeletal injuries, raise the body's temperature in preparation for activity, and stretch the major muscle groups. However, a warm-up does not release hydrogen from myoglobin. Myoglobin binds oxygen, not hydrogen.

PHYSICAL EDUCATION

135. Which is not a benefit of cooling down? (Rigorous) (Skill 9.1)
    A. Preventing dizziness.
    B. Redistributing circulation.
    C. Removing lactic acid.
    D. Removing myoglobin.

(D.) Cooling down helps the body to regain blood circulation and to remove lactic acid. It also prevents dizziness, which may occur after extensive exercises. The only thing that cooling down does not support is removing myoglobin. However, it can help myoglobin get a strong hold in the muscles.

136. Overloading for muscle strength includes all of the following except: (Rigorous) (Skill 9.1)
    A. Lifting heart rate to an intense level.
    B. Lifting weights every other day.
    C. Lifting with high resistance and low reps.
    D. Lifting 60% to 90% of assessed muscle strength.

(A.) Overloading muscle strength is possible by lifting the weights every other day or by lifting weights with high resistance and low repetition. Overloading does not cause or require an intense increase in heart rate. However, overloading has many other possibilities.

137. Which of the following applies the concept of progression? (Rigorous) (Skill 9.1)
    A. Beginning a stretching program every day.
    B. Beginning a stretching program with 3 sets of reps.
    C. Beginning a stretching program with ballistic stretching.
    D. Beginning a stretching program holding stretches for 15 seconds and work up to holding stretches for 60 seconds.

(D.) Progression is the process of starting an exercise program slowly and cautiously before proceeding to more rigorous training. Answer D is the only answer that exemplifies progression.

138. Which of following overload principles does not apply to improving body composition? (Average Rigor) (Skill 9.1)
    A. Aerobic exercise three times per week.
    B. Aerobic exercise at a low intensity.
    C. Aerobic exercise for about an hour.
    D. Aerobic exercise in intervals of high intensity.

(A.) To improve body composition, a person should engage in aerobic exercise daily, not three times per week. However, an individual can do aerobics for at least half an hour daily, he/she can exercise at a low intensity, or he/she can train with intervals of high intensity.

139. Which of the following principles of progression applies to improving muscle endurance? (Average Rigor) (Skill 9.1)
   A. Lifting weights every day.
   B. Lifting weights at 20% to 30% of assessed muscle strength.
   C. Lifting weights with low resistance and low reps.
   D. Lifting weights starting at 60% of assessed muscle strength.

(B.) To improve muscle endurance, a person should lift weights at 20 to 30% of the assessed muscle strength. Lifting weights daily is counterproductive because it does not allow for adequate rest. In addition, lifting at 60% of the assessed muscle strength can damage the muscle.

XAMonline, INC. 21 Orient Ave. Melrose, MA 02176

Toll Free number 800-509-4128

TO ORDER Fax 781-662-9268 OR www.XAMonline.com

WEST SERIES

PO# Store/School:

Address 1:

Address 2 (Ship to other):

City, State Zip

Credit card number _____-_____-_____-_____ expiration_____

EMAIL _____

PHONE FAX

ISBN	TITLE	Qty	Retail	Total
978-1-58197-638-0	WEST-B Basic Skills		$27.95	
978-1-58197-609-0	WEST-E Biology 0235		$59.95	
978-1-58197-693-9	WEST-E Chemistry 0245		$59.95	
978-1-58197-566-6	WEST-E Designated World Language: French Sample Test 0173		$15.00	
978-1-58197-557-4	WEST-E Designated World Language: Spanish 0191		$59.95	
978-1-58197-614-4	WEST-E Elementary Education 0014		$28.95	
978-1-58197-636-6	WEST-E English Language Arts 0041		$59.95	
978-1-58197-634-2	WEST-E General Science 0435		$59.95	
978-1-58197-637-3	WEST-E Health & Fitness 0856		$59.95	
978-1-58197-635-9	WEST-E Library Media 0310		$59.95	
978-1-58197-674-8	WEST-E Mathematics 0061		$59.95	
978-1-58197-556-7	WEST-E Middle Level Humanities 0049, 0089		$59.95	
978-1-58197-043-2	WEST-E Physics 0265		$59.95	
978-1-58197-563-5	WEST-E Reading/Literacy 0300		$59.95	
978-1-58197-552-9	WEST-E Social Studies 0081		$59.95	
978-1-58197-639-7	WEST-E Special Education 0353		$73.50	
978-1-58197-633-5	WEST-E Visual Arts Sample Test 0133		$15.00	
	SUBTOTAL		Ship	$8.25
	FOR PRODUCT PRICES VISIT WWW.XAMONLINE.COM		**TOTAL**	

www.ingramcontent.com/pod-product-compliance
Lightning Source LLC
Chambersburg PA
CBHW080538300426
44111CB00017B/2791